Better Homes and Gardens

CHRISTMAS

FROM THE HEART

Tea for two,
from me to you!

Better Homes and Gardens®

CHRISTMAS

FROM THE HEART®

Volume 12

Better Homes and Gardens® Creative Collection™
Des Moines, Iowa

Contents

Holly and Berries

WITH THE CRISP AROMA of its dark green leaves and the jolly round features of its red berries, holly is nature's essential Christmas decorating accent. Paired with miniature silver-plated pieces including teacups and saucers, sugar bowls, cream pitchers, and serving trays, you can make your own high-style statement on a tree, wreath, or garland, *opposite*. Adorn velvet-covered balls, star-shape cutouts, *above*, and pinecones with holly and berries for ornaments rich in red-and-green tradition.

Combine the luxury of beautiful red velvet with the simple elegance of holly and berries to make a beautiful ornament, *above*. Starting with a plain plastic-foam ball, use two pieces of velvet to cover the surface and then embellish it with a wreath of holly and berries secured along the seam.

Make creative use of a miniature silver sugar bowl or a cream pitcher, *opposite*, by inserting a piece of plastic foam inside and tucking sprigs of holly and berries into it.

Use miniature silver serving pieces or other shiny items you already own to add glitz and glamour to your holiday arrangements.

Don't get your polishing cloth out quite yet—there's no need when you use miniature silver-plated serving pieces to personalize a wreath and garland, *opposite*. Small teapots, creamers, cups, and saucers are the perfect size for positioning among berry sprays and sheer red ribbon.

Pinecones drip with updated elegance on the tree *above* and the garland *opposite* with the addition of holly, berries, and ribbon. Holes drilled into the top of each pinecone help anchor the embellishments.

Star Ornament

Shown on page 7.

YOU WILL NEED

- Tracing paper
- 5×5-inch square of 1⁄8-inch thick foam-core board
- Red velvet paper
- 8 to16 miniature holly leaves with sprigs of miniature berries
- Medium red berry clusters
- 6 to 12 large red berries
- 6-inch length of 1⁄8-inch-wide red gimp
- Crafts glue
- Glue gun and hotmelt adhesive
- Deckle-edge paper scissors

INSTRUCTIONS

Trace the star pattern *below* and cut it out. Cut out one foam-core star with sharp scissors. Then use deckle-edge paper scissors to cut out two red stars just slightly larger than the foam-core star. Use crafts glue to attach one red star to the bottom of the foam-core star. To make the hanger, form a loop from the gimp; glue the looped gimp ends to the top of one point of the foam-core star.

Glue the other red star to the top of the foam-core star, covering the ends of the gimp hanger. Hot-glue individual holly leaves to the top points of the star (or, if you prefer, decorate both sides of the star for a reversible ornament). Hot-glue the medium berry clusters onto the star's surface so it's completely covered by leaves and berries. Glue three individual leaves and a berry cluster in the center of the star. Hot-glue the larger berries randomly among the medium-size berries.

Sugar and Cream Ornaments

Shown on page 10.

YOU WILL NEED

- 2-inch cube of plastic foam
- Utility knife
- 2½-inch-tall silver-plate cream pitcher or sugar bowl
- Miniature holly and berry sprays
- Two or three large holly leaves with berries
- Sprigs of berry clusters
- Two olive green velvet leaves
- Crafts glue
- Florist's tape
- Glue gun and hotmelt adhesive
- Florist's wire

INSTRUCTIONS

Using a utility knife, trim the plastic-foam cube as necessary to fit firmly inside the cream pitcher or sugar bowl. Insert the plastic foam into the creamer or sugar bowl.

Glue the larger holly leaves and the velvet leaves into the plastic foam near the center, allowing one leaf to extend over the edge of the creamer or sugar bowl along the side front edge of the bowl or pitcher. Glue individual miniature holly leaves along the remaining edges.

Arrange the miniature holly and berry leaves with the larger leaves, and glue them into the plastic foam. If necessary, wrap the sprays with florist's tape so that the sprays fan nicely in the arrangement. Hot-glue the larger berries and berry clusters within the holly sprays.

Use florist's wire to firmly attach the ornament to the tree branch, using other branches to help support the ornament.

Pinecone Ornament

Shown above and on page 11.

YOU WILL NEED

- Large pinecone
- Two sprays of miniature holly and berries
- Three large holly leaves with berries
- 6-inch length of ½-inch-wide red ribbon
- ½ yard of 1-inch-wide double-face red satin ribbon
- Florist's wire
- Florist's tape
- E6000 adhesive
- Cordless screw-gun drill
- 1½-inch drill bit

INSTRUCTIONS

Drill three 1-inch deep holes into the top of the pinecone so that the holes are positioned equally apart (in a triangle formation). Fold the narrow ribbon in half to form a loop; tie the ends together. Glue the knot into the center top hole. Glue a double-leaf sprig of the larger holly and berries into the top hole with the ribbon loop.

Wrap the stems of a group of small holly leaves and berries together with florist's tape; make two groupings. Insert the holly groupings into the remaining two drilled holes.

Loop the wider ribbon into a bow; wrap a piece of florist's wire around the bow center. Trim the bow tails; glue the wire into one of the holes. Fill in with additional holly and berries.

Wreathed Ball Ornament

Shown below and on page 8.

YOU WILL NEED

- One 3-inch Styrofoam plastic-foam ball
- ⅝ yard of ⅜-inch-wide red velvet ribbon
- 5×10-inch piece of sparkly red velvet fabric
- Miniature holly and berry sprays
- Five large berries
- Sprigs of red berry clusters
- Straight pins
- Glue gun and hotmelt adhesive
- Green florist's tape

INSTRUCTIONS

Cut out two 4½-inch-diameter circles of velvet fabric. Cover half the plastic-foam ball with one velvet circle, pinning the outer edge of the circle to the ball. Cover the other half of the ball with the second velvet circle, making sure the outer fabric edges meet.

Cover the raw fabric edges with the ⅜-inch-wide red velvet ribbon. Pull the ribbon snugly against the ball shape; trim the excess ribbon, and overlap ends, securing the ribbon in place with a pin at the center top of the ball. Center and pin the remaining 9-inch length of velvet ribbon to the top of the ball.

Pin or hot-glue individual holly leaves around the ball circumference, covering the velvet ribbon. Pin 3-leaf sprays of holly leaves along with the individual holly leaves. If necessary, bind the stems of the 3-leaf sprays with pieces of florist's tape so that the sprays lay better around the ball. Hot-glue the larger berries and berry clusters among the holly leaves, hiding the stems and glue under the leaves.

All designs by Mary Jo Hiney

Earth Angels

ENTER A BLISSFUL WORLD where delicate angels flutter among doves and inspirational images shine in the Christmas lights. These heavenly inspired creations offer an uplifting approach to decorating.

Reminiscent of vintage blown-glass ornaments, the oversized finial decorations *above* are created from plastic-foam balls and wooden shapes decoupaged with tissue paper and lace. The body of the angel *opposite* takes shape with the adaptation of a wooden egg, candle cup, and a pair of dollhouse railings.

If you yearn for a tree decked with abundant beauty without sacrificing the true meaning of the season, the ornaments on the tree *opposite* may be just what you've been searching for. Resplendent in shades of soft white, lavender, and pink, timeless ornaments include pretty prayer envelopes, wispy angels, romantic wool-felt hearts, majestic emblems, and elegant shadow boxes for holding mementos.

Paper—in its many forms—makes each ornament *above* unique. Light and airy vellum, cut into petal shapes, forms the skirt of the angel, and a page from a stained-glass coloring book is the basis for the hand-colored "window" ornament. Torn watercolor paper takes flight as a graceful dove.

Vintage sweaters—too pretty to part with—get a second lease on life when selected beading and embroidery details are highlighted for a pair of Christmas stockings, *above*. Interesting buttons, once-functional plackets, and small pockets reincarnated to hold Christmas greens also make each stocking one-of-a-kind.

Delicate baby's-breath, twiggy white berries, and translucent skeleton leaves combine on a painted white grapevine circle to create the snowy look of the wreath *opposite*. Frosted glass balls and small sheer bows scattered around the wreath dress it up for the holidays.

After Christmas, dress up this wreath with other ribbons and accents for special occasions or year-round use.

Decoupage Angel

Shown below and on page 16.

YOU WILL NEED

- Wood pieces: 1-inch-tall candle cup for the base, 4½-inch-tall turned finial for the body, ¾-inch-diameter wheel for the halo, and two 2⅝-inch-tall dollhouse railings for the arms
- Drill; 5⁄64-inch drill bit
- Tacky glue
- Scrap of muslin fabric
- Papers: sage green, ecru embossed fibrous, and blush patterned tissue
- Mod Podge decoupage medium
- Sponge brush
- Dried leaf stem
- Glue gun and hotmelt adhesive
- 5-inch length of 24-gauge green florist's wire
- Needle-nose pliers
- Wire cutters
- Two gold skeleton leaves
- 12-inch length of narrow gold cording

INSTRUCTIONS

Make a hole through the shoulder area of the turned finial with the 5⁄64-inch drill bit. Also, use the drill bit to make a hole through the wider end of each dollhouse railings.

Turn the candle cup upside down and glue the bottom to the wide end of the turned finial with tacky glue. Glue the wheel to the narrow end of the finial for the halo. Let the glue dry thoroughly.

Tear a piece of muslin to cover the candle cup. Use the sponge brush to apply a thin coat of decoupage medium to the cup. Smooth the muslin scrap onto the wet surface. Use your fingers to smooth the fabric in place, removing any bubbles.

Tear pieces of sage green paper for the bottom section of the finial, pieces of ecru embossed paper for the large center section of the finial, and pieces of blush tissue paper for the head, halo, and arms. Working with one section at a time, apply a thin coat of decoupage medium. Place the paper pieces onto the wet surface one at a time, slightly overlapping the edges. Gently press the pieces in place, smoothing to remove bubbles and adhere the edges. When the wood pieces are completely covered, coat them entirely with decoupage medium.

Tear an additional scrap of muslin for the lower body and a tiny piece for the neck. Adhere the larger pieces around the body between the sage green and ecru embossed papers. Wrap the tiny piece around the neck and knot at the center front; trim the ends.

When the decoupage medium is completely dry, hot-glue the dried leaf stem around the body where the cup attaches to the bottom of the finial.

To attach the arms, coil one end of the florist's wire two times around the tip of the needle-nose pliers. Slip the opposite end first through the hole in one arm, then through the shoulders of the finial, and finally through the hole in the second arm. Pull the wire so the arms are next to the body and trim the wire ¼ inch beyond the second arm. Coil the wire end to secure the arms.

For the wings, hot-glue the stem end of the skeleton leaves to the center back of the angel so the top edges of the wings are at the bottom of the head. Glue a torn piece of embossed paper over the wings to cover the stem ends and to protect the fragile leaves.

For the hanging loop, knot the narrow cording snugly around the area between the halo and head so that the ends are even. Knot the ends together, forming a loop.

Christmas Story Emblem Ornament

Shown above and on page 16.

YOU WILL NEED

- Tracing paper
- 5×8-inch piece of crescent board
- Scrapbook papers: lavender tone-on-tone, copper hammered metallic, parchment, and pale pink embossed vellum
- Straight- and deckle-edge paper scissors
- 12-inch length of 18-gauge copper wire
- Needle-nose pliers
- Masking tape
- Glue stick
- Brown fine-tip permanent marker
- ½ yard of 3⁄16-inch-diameter periwinkle twisted cording
- Mauve rosebud
- Glue gun and hotmelt adhesive
- Wire cutters

INSTRUCTIONS

Trace the emblem patterns *below* onto tracing paper. Cut out the pattern pieces. Trace the large emblem twice onto the lavender paper. Trace the medium emblem twice onto the crescent board and once onto the copper hammered metallic paper. Trace the small emblem once onto the parchment paper and once onto the vellum. Use the deckle-edge scissors to cut out the vellum emblem. Use the straight-edge scissors to cut out all remaining emblems.

Glue the two crescent board emblems together. For the hanger, bend the wire to fit between the top corners of the layered crescent-board emblems, using the needle-nose pliers to make random small loops and to coil each end. Tape the hanger to one side of the layered emblems at the top corners of the ornament front. Glue a lavender emblem to each side of the crescent board. Center and glue the copper emblem on the ornament front.

Use the brown fine-tip marker to write a portion of the Christmas story onto the parchment emblem. You might want to practice first on scrap paper. Center and glue the parchment emblem on the copper emblem. Center and glue the vellum emblem onto the parchment emblem.

Beginning and ending at the top center, hot-glue periwinkle cording to the edges of the ornament in the space between the lavender emblems. Hot-glue the rosebud to the top center of the vellum emblem.

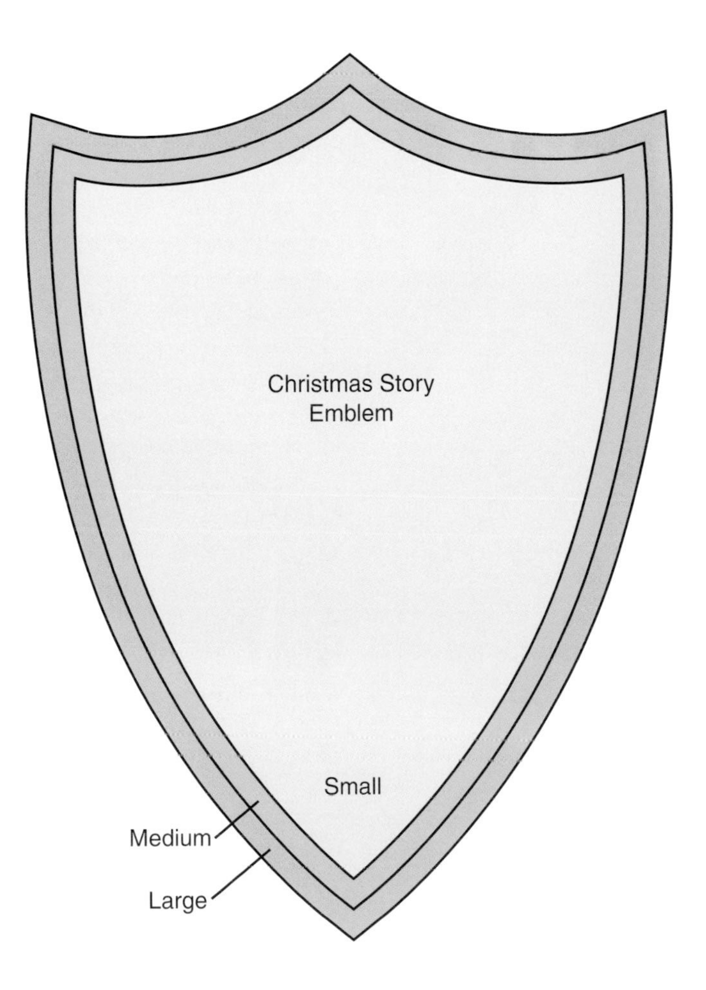

Baby's Breath Wreath

Shown on page 19.

YOU WILL NEED

- 14-inch grapevine wreath
- Spray paint: Krylon Buttercream
- 12- or 14-inch white berry wreath
- 26-gauge silver wire
- Wire cutters
- Four or more bunches of natural white gypsophila
- 2-inch-diameter frosted glass bulbs (we used 16 of them)
- One or two packages of off-white skeleton leaves

10-foot length of crystal-with-green-leaf-beaded garland
Glue gun and hotmelt adhesive
6 yards of 5/8-inch-wide pale green sheer ribbon
Florist's picks

INSTRUCTIONS

Spray the grapevine wreath with the Buttercream paint; let the paint dry. Position the white berry wreath on the grapevine wreath; wire in place.

Separate the gypsophila into small bunches. Wire the small bunches around the inner edge of the berry wreath, overlapping to cover the ends. Arrange the glass bulbs on the wreath. When pleased with the arrangement, wire the bulbs in place. Hot-glue skeleton leaves around the wreath, filling in any open spaces and tucking the leaves between the layers.

Drape the garland around the wreath; wire in place. Make a pale green sheer ribbon bow with 10-inch-long tails. Wire the bow to a florist's pick and insert at the center top of the wreath. To make a ribbon pick, fold the sheer ribbon back and forth, creating four 2-inch-long loops on each side. Wire the center of the folded ribbon to a florist's pick and stick the pick in the wreath. Repeat to make four or five ribbon picks.

Finial Ornaments

Shown top right and on page 14.

YOU WILL NEED

For each ornament:
12-inch length of 1/4-inch-diameter wooden dowel
Assorted sizes and shapes of Styrofoam plastic-foam pieces, such as 2-, 2½-, and 4-inch-diameter balls; a 6-inch tree; and a 6×4-inch egg
Assorted sizes and shapes of wood pieces such as 1-inch-diameter wheels, 1-inch-long beads, 1-inch-diameter candle cups, and 3/4×1/2- and 3/4×2½-inch finials
Drill and 1/4-inch drill bit
Plastic-foam glue
One sheet of ecru patterned tissue paper
Mod Podge decoupage medium
Sponge brush
Ecru paint
Sponge
Scraps of vintage lace
1 yard of 1/4-inch-wide ecru satin ribbon
Crafts glue
Small lavender dried rosebuds
Mirror pieces: 1/2-inch square, 1/2-inch round, and 1×3/4-inch oval
Crystal beads: 6-millimeter round and small heart
Straight pins
5/8-inch-diameter iridescent round sequins with a top hole

INSTRUCTIONS

Arrange the plastic-foam shapes and wood pieces to fit on the 12-inch length of dowel, referring to the photograph *top right* for ideas. Make holes through the plastic-foam shapes and drill holes through the wood pieces if necessary. Slide the pieces on the dowel, gluing the pieces together and to the dowel with plastic-foam glue. Let the glue dry.

Tear the sheet of tissue paper into small irregular-shape pieces. Use the sponge brush to apply a thin coat of decoupage medium to the assembled finial, working with a small section at a time. Place a piece of tissue paper on the wet surface. Use your fingers to gently press the paper in place, smoothing from the center out to

remove bubbles and adhere the edges. Add additional tissue-paper pieces, one at a time and slightly overlapping the edges, until the wet surface is covered. Continue working a section at a time until the finial is covered with tissue-paper pieces; let dry. Coat entire finial with decoupage medium.

When the decoupage medium is completely dry, use the ecru paint to sponge-paint the finial. When dry, adhere pieces of lace to the plastic-foam shapes with decoupage medium.

For the hanging loop, glue the center of the satin ribbon to the top of the finial. Knot and tie a bow in the ribbon about 4 inches above the finial.

Decorate the finial as desired. Glue rosebuds and mirrors in place. Use straight pins or glue to attach the beads. Attach the sequins with straight pins.

Paper Dove Ornament

Shown on page 17.

YOU WILL NEED

- Tracing paper; pencil
- One sheet of watercolor paper
- Small scissors
- 12-inch length of 24-gauge silver wire
- Needle-nose pliers
- Beads: size 8/0 pale aqua seed, size 11/0 crystal silver seed, four 4-millimeter crystal rondelle, three green leaves, and one 6×10-millimeter crystal teardrop
- Wire cutters
- Transparent tape; glue stick

INSTRUCTIONS

Trace the dove patterns *below* onto tracing paper; cut out. Use a pencil to lightly trace one base, two bodies, two large wings, and one small wing onto watercolor paper. Carefully tear the base shape along the pencil lines. Use a small scissors to cut out the remaining pieces. Referring to the photograph on *page 17*, freehand-cut curved slivers into the bottom edge of each wing. Erase pencil lines.

Coil one end of the silver wire four times around the tip of the needle-nose pliers. Thread an assortment of beads, including the leaf beads and two rondelle beads, onto the wire to measure approximately $3\frac{1}{4}$ inches. Slide the beads up against the coil. Position the wire on the dove base with the beaded area ending at the beak. Bring the wire across the base to exit between the wings. Tape the wire to the base from the end of the beaded section to the wings.

For the hanger, thread an assortment of beads, including the remaining rondelle and the teardrop, onto the

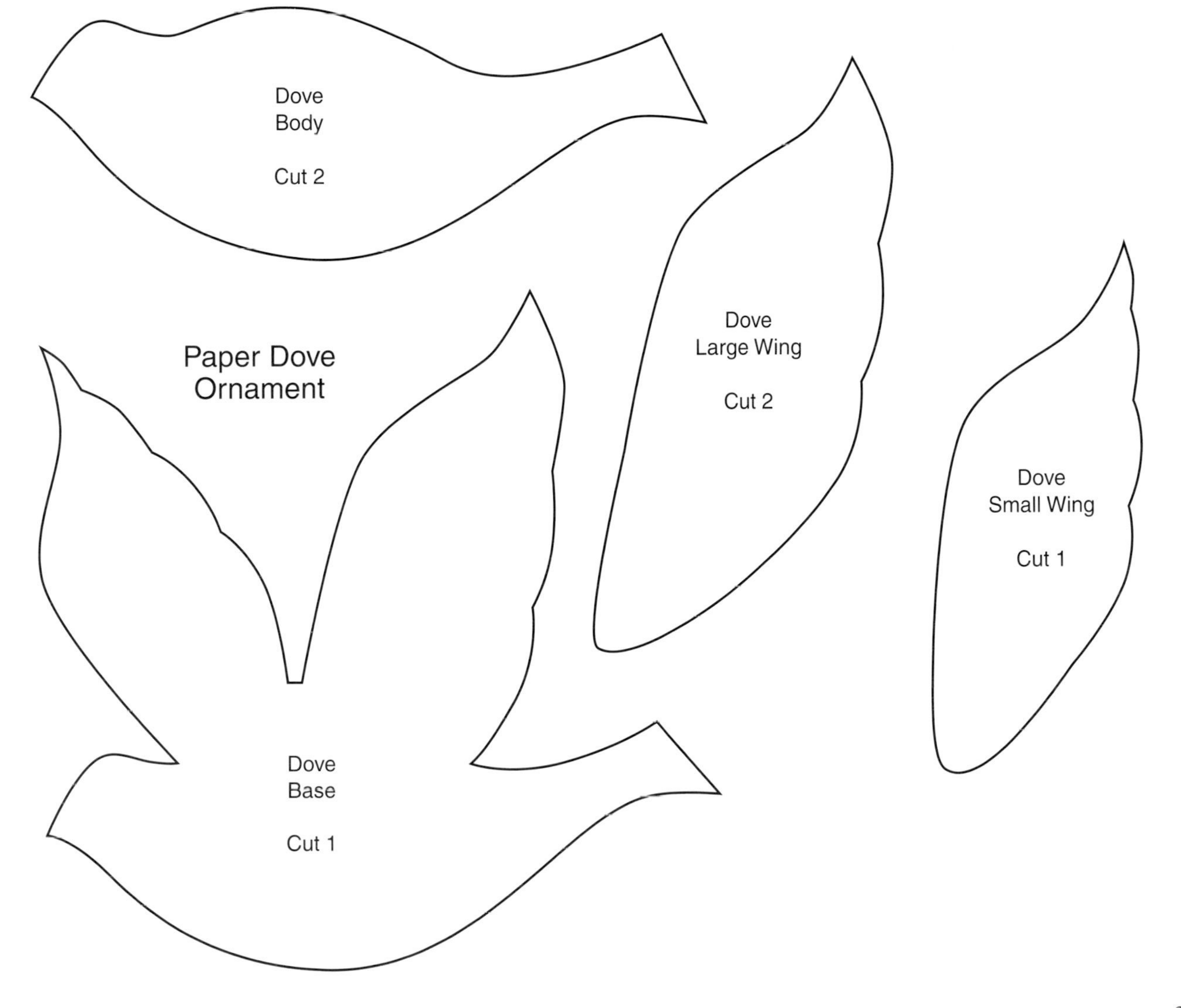

wire to measure $3\frac{3}{4}$ inches. Coil the wire four times around the tip of the pliers next to the last bead. Trim the excess wire. Glue in order the small wing, one body, and one large wing onto the front of the base, covering the unbeaded area of the wire. Glue the second large wing and then a body onto the back of the base. Bend the hanger into a fishhook shape.

Prayer Envelope Ornament

Shown below and on page 16.

YOU WILL NEED

- Tracing paper
- Pencil
- One $8\frac{1}{2}$×11-inch sheet of off-white with taupe vellum
- Scoring tool
- Glue stick
- $\frac{1}{4}$ yard of 4-millimeter rust silk ribbon
- Large-eye embroidery needle
- Olive-green brush-tip marker
- $\frac{1}{8}$×12-inch strip of copper metallic paper
- Scraps of three coordinating scrapbook papers

INSTRUCTIONS

Trace the envelope pattern *opposite* onto tracing paper; cut it out. Use a pencil to lightly trace around the pattern onto the vellum. Cut out the envelope shape and score it as indicated on the pattern. Fold in the side flaps and fold up the bottom flap. Glue the overlapped edges together.

Thread the needle with the ribbon; knot one end. Working from inside the envelope, pull the needle through the dot in the top flap of the envelope as indicated on the pattern until the knots rests against the paper. Bring the ribbon back through the top flat at the second dot. Remove the needle and knot the ribbon end, forming a hanging loop.

Use the olive-green marker to outline the front flap edges. Tightly coil the $\frac{1}{8}$-inch strip of copper metallic paper. Let the coil loosen into a 1-inch-diameter circle.

Glue the outer end to the outer surface of the circle. Pinch one end of the circle, forming a teardrop shape. Rub the glue stick on one side of the teardrop shape and press onto the front flap.

From the scraps of coordinating papers, cut one $2\frac{3}{8}$×$3\frac{3}{8}$-inch rectangle, one 2×3-inch rectangle, and one $1\frac{1}{2}$×$2\frac{1}{2}$-inch rectangle. Center and glue the layers together from smallest to largest. Insert the layered papers in the envelope. Write a prayer or wish on the card, and insert into the envelope.

Stained Glass Window Ornament

Shown on page 17.

YOU WILL NEED

- Small pewter picture frame
- Stained glass coloring book
- Pencil
- Brush-tip markers
- $\frac{1}{4}$-inch-wide strips of heavyweight cardboard
- Thick crafts glue
- 12-inch length of 1-inch-wide coral bias-cut silk ribbon

INSTRUCTIONS

Take the glass out of the frame (the frame backing and stand won't be used). Center the glass over the desired area of a coloring book page and use a pencil to trace around the glass. Color the area inside the traced lines with brush-tip markers. Cut out the design on the traced lines.

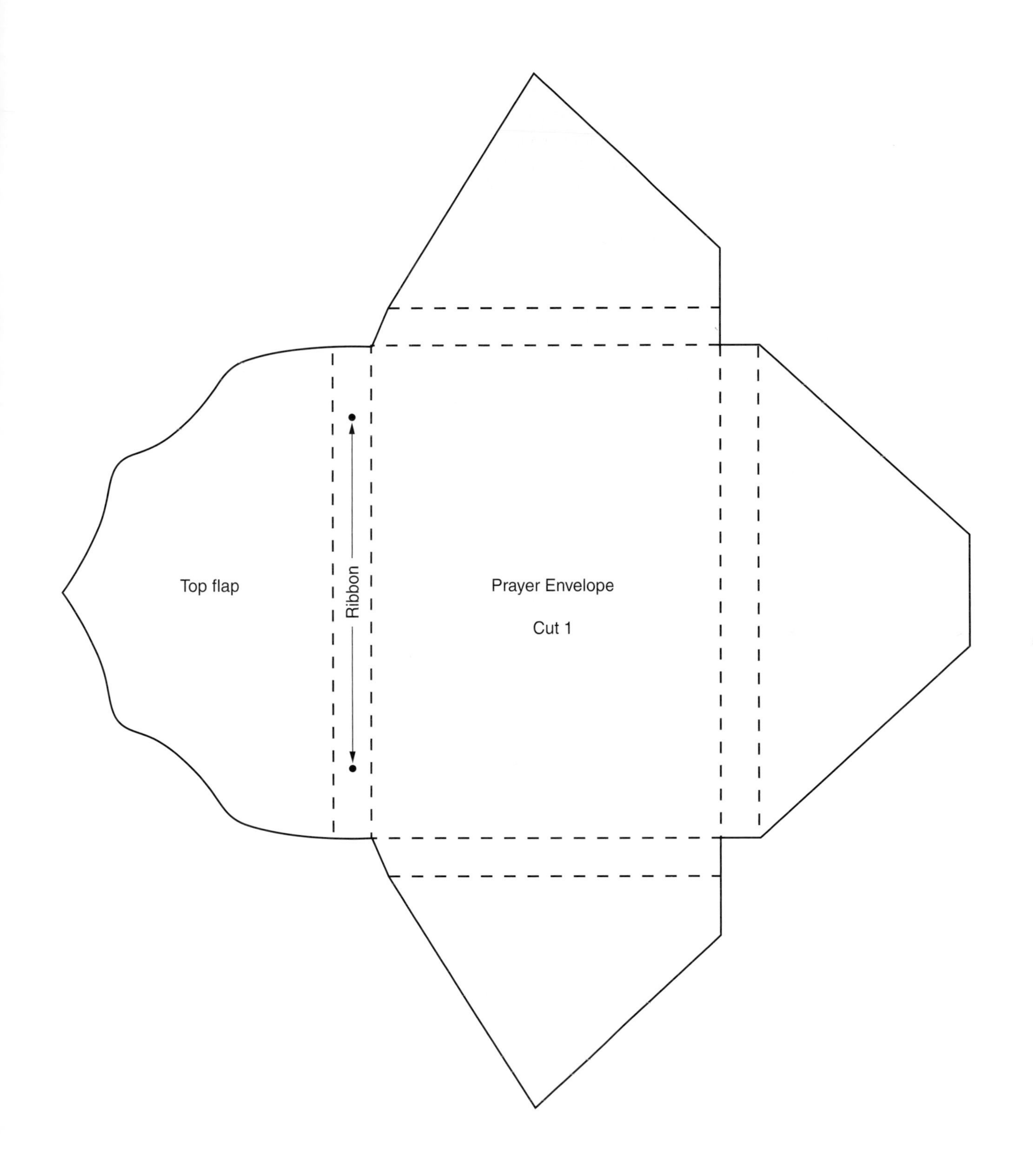
Top flap
Ribbon
Prayer Envelope
Cut 1

Clean the glass. Insert the glass and then the design in the frame. Cut a strip of cardboard for each edge of the frame opening. Glue the strips together and to the back of the frame, anchoring the design.

For the hanging loop, thread the ribbon ends through the top corners of the frame and knot the ribbon ends around the center of the ribbon.

Rose Petal and Vellum Angel

Shown far right and on page 17.

YOU WILL NEED

- Wood pieces: 1-inch-diameter wheel for base, 2½-inch egg for lower body, 1¼-inch-tall candle cup for upper body, two ½-inch-diameter wheels for neck and halo, 1-inch-long egg for head, six 6-millimeter round beads for arms, and four 15-millimeter oval beads for arms
- Drill; 5⁄64-inch drill bit
- Short nails and hammer
- Tacky glue
- Gesso
- Linen acrylic paint
- Paintbrush
- Papers: blush patterned tissue, light green leaf-print vellum, and pale rose embossed vellum
- Mod Podge decoupage medium
- Sponge brush
- Tracing paper
- Small blush eyelets
- Eyelet tool
- ¼ yard of 1-inch-wide ivory bias-cut silk ribbon with apricot edging
- Preserved baby's breath
- Glue gun and hotmelt adhesive
- 18-inch length of 24- or 26-gauge silver wire
- Wire cutters
- Beads: silver bugle, size 8/0 pale aqua seed, four 8-millimeter pale green round, two 8-millimeter clear round, and two 6×10-millimeter crystal teardrop
- E6000 adhesive
- 10-inch length of 24-gauge green florist's wire
- Needle-nose pliers
- 12-inch length of gold narrow cording

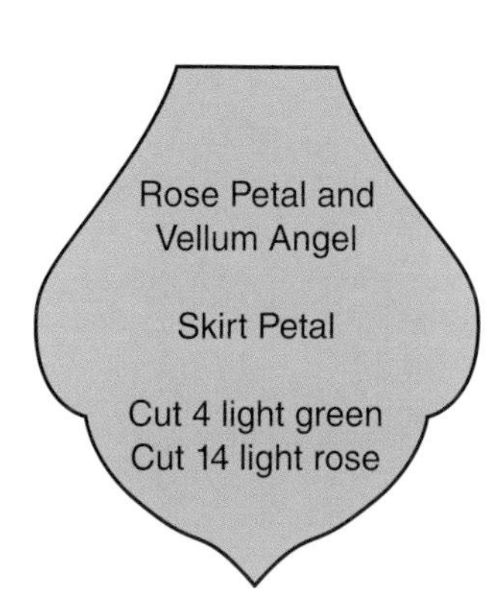

INSTRUCTIONS

Turn the candle cup upside down for the upper body. Make a hole through opposite sides of the cup in the shoulder area with the 5⁄64-inch drill bit for the arms. Drill an additional hole about ¼ inch behind each armhole for the wings. To make nailing easier, drill a hole straight down into the pointed end of each egg.

Nail and glue the 1-inch-diameter wheel to the pointed end of the large egg. Glue the open end of the candle cup to the rounded end of the large egg. Nail and glue a ½-inch-diameter wheel to the pointed end of the small egg. Glue the remaining ½-inch-diameter wheel to the rounded end of the small egg. Allow the glue to dry thoroughly.

Apply a coat of gesso to the candle cup and neck wheel for texture; let the gesso dry. Apply two coats of linen

paint to the 1-inch-diameter wheel, large egg, candle cup, and neck, letting the paint dry between coats.

Tear small pieces of blush patterned tissue paper. Use the sponge brush to apply a thin coat of decoupage medium to the head and halo. Place the paper pieces onto the wet surface one at a time, slightly overlapping the edges. Gently press each piece in place, smoothing to remove bubbles and adhere the edges. Coat the entire papered surfaces with decoupage medium and let dry.

Trace the skirt petal pattern *left* onto tracing paper. Cut out the pattern piece. Trace the pattern four times onto the light green leaf-print vellum and fourteen times onto the pale rose embossed vellum. Cut out the petals. Glue the four light green petals around the large egg so the bottom tips just reach the 1-inch-diameter wheel, placing one at the center front, one at the center back, and one at each side. Overlap and glue seven pale rose petals around the egg about ½ inch above the previous petals. Apply a blush eyelet near the center bottom point of the remaining pale rose petals, using the eyelet tool. Glue the remaining seven petals overlapping around the angel's waist.

Snugly wrap the bias-cut ribbon around the candle cup below the armholes for the bodice. Knot the ribbon ends together at the center back. Hot-glue baby's breath to the bottom of the 1-inch diameter wheel and around the neck.

For the wings, cut the silver wire in half. Following the same pattern for each wing, thread the beads onto the wire lengths to measure 6 inches. Shape each wing, twisting the wires together below the beads. Trim the twisted area to measure ½ inch. Insert and glue the twisted wire area in the predrilled wing holes with the E6000 adhesive.

For the arms, coil one end of the florist's wire two times around the tip of the needle-nose pliers. Thread three round and two oval wood beads onto the opposite end of the wire, alternating the beads. Slide the beads down the wire to rest on the coil. Slip the wire through the predrilled armholes in the candle cup. Thread the remaining beads onto the wire in the same pattern. Pull the wire so the bead arms are next to the body and trim the wire ¼ inch beyond the last bead; then coil the wire end to secure the arms.

For the hanging loop, knot the narrow cording snugly around the area between the halo and head so that the ends are even. Knot the ends together, forming a loop.

Shell Angel

Shown below and on page 16.

YOU WILL NEED

- Wood pieces: 2 ¼×2¾-inch flowerpot for the skirt, 1-inch-tall spool for the upper body, 1-inch-tall finial for the neck and head, ½-inch-diameter wheel for the halo, six 6-millimeter beads for the arms, and two 15-millimeter oval beads for the arms
- Drill; 5⁄64-inch drill bit
- Tacky glue
- Gesso
- Paintbrush
- Acrylic paint: oyster pearl
- Blush patterned tissue paper
- Mod Podge decoupage medium
- Sponge brush
- Seashells in assorted shapes measuring ⅜–1 inch
- Glue gun and hotmelt adhesive
- 24-gauge green florist's wire
- Needle-nose pliers
- E6000 adhesive
- 12-inch length of gold narrow cording

INSTRUCTIONS

Make a hole through opposite sides of the spool in the shoulder area with the 5⁄64-inch drill bit for the arms. Drill an additional hole about ¼ inch behind each armhole for the wings.

Turn the flowerpot upside down for the skirt. Glue the bottom of the spool to the flat end of the flowerpot. Center and glue the finial to the top of the spool. Glue the wheel to the top of the finial. Let the glue dry thoroughly.

Apply a coat of gesso to the spool and the neck area of the finial; let the gesso dry. Apply two coats of oyster pearl paint to the flowerpot, spool, and neck area of finial, letting the paint dry between coats.

Tear small pieces of the blush tissue paper. Use the sponge brush to apply a thin coat of the decoupage medium to the head area of the finial and the halo. Place the paper pieces on the wet surface one at a time, slightly overlapping the edges. Gently press each piece in place, smoothing to

remove bubbles and adhere the edges. Coat all the papered surfaces with the decoupage medium and let dry.

Beginning at the top of the skirt with the smaller seashells, hot-glue the shells to the flowerpot in rows, leaving the larger shells for the rim of the pot.

For the arms, coil one end of the florist's wire two times around the tip of the needle-nose pliers. Thread two round, one oval, and one round wood bead onto the opposite end of the wire. Slide the beads down the wire to rest on the coil. Slip the wire through the predrilled armholes in the spool. Thread the remaining beads onto the wire, reversing the pattern. Pull the wire so the bead arms are next to the body and trim the wire ¼ inch beyond the last bead. Coil the wire end to secure the arms.

For the wings, cut two 8-inch lengths of florist's wire. Following the same pattern for each wing, shape each wire into a small wing. Twist the wire ends together at the base of the wing. Trim the twisted area to measure ½ inch. Insert and glue the twisted area in the predrilled wingholes with the E6000 adhesive.

For the hanging loop, knot the narrow cording snugly around the area between the halo and head so the ends are even. Knot the ends together, forming a loop.

Shadow Box Ornament

Shown below and on page 16.

YOU WILL NEED

2¾x3½-inch oval box, base only
4-inch square of crescent board
Drill; 5⁄64-inch drill bit
9-inch length of narrow gold cording
Patterned scrapbook paper
Crafts glue
2×3-inch oval mirror
E6000 adhesive
Preserved baby's breath
Glue gun and hotmelt adhesive
1½ yards of 1-inch-wide taupe/green bias-cut ribbon
¾ yard of 7-millimeter coral ribbon
Seashell to fit inside box

INSTRUCTIONS

Trace the bottom of the box base onto the crescent board. Cut out the crescent board oval ⅛ inch beyond the traced line for the ornament back. Use the 5⁄64-inch drill bit to make two holes ¼ inch apart at the top center of the base for the hanging loop. Working from inside the base, thread the gold cording ends through the holes; knot the ends together for the loop.

Trace the crescent-board oval onto the wrong side of the scrapbook paper. Cut out the paper oval ½ inch beyond the traced line. Use crafts glue to glue the paper to the crescent board oval, wrapping the paper around the edges. Cut a strip of scrapbook paper to cover the inner sides of the base; then glue it in place.

Center and glue the mirror to the inside bottom of the base with E6000 adhesive. Hot-glue baby's breath around the inner bottom edges of the base, covering the mirror edges.

Snugly wrap the bias-cut ribbon several times around the outside of the base, allowing some ribbon to extend over the top edge of the base. Glue ribbon ends in place.

Glue the 7-millimeter ribbon to the bottom of the base in a back and forth diagonal manner, creating ribbon folds that extend a scant ¼ inch beyond the edge of the base. Glue the paper-covered oval back to the bottom of the base with wrong sides facing. Glue the shell centered on the mirror.

Fringe Angel

Shown opposite and on page 15.

YOU WILL NEED

½ yard of 5-inch-long white rayon fringe
Café au lait cold-water fabric dye
Wood pieces: two 1¼-inch-tall candle cups for the body, ¾-inch-diameter wheel for the neck, 1½-inch egg for the head, and two 2⅝-inch-tall dollhouse railings for the arms
Drill; 5⁄64-inch drill bit
Short nail and hammer
Tacky glue
Gesso
Linen acrylic paint
Paintbrush
Blush patterned tissue paper

- Mod Podge decoupage medium
- Sponge brush
- Scrap of Chantilly lace
- Preserved light green candytuft
- One lavender rosebud
- Glue gun and hotmelt adhesive
- 5-inch length of 24-gauge green florist's wire
- Needle-nose pliers
- Wire cutters
- Six pale mauve feathers
- 12-inch length of gold narrow cording

INSTRUCTIONS

Cut the rayon fringe in half. Dye the fringe in the cold-water dye until the desired color is achieved, following the manufacturer's instructions. Set aside to dry.

Turn one candle cup upside down for the upper body. Make a hole through opposite sides of the cup in the shoulder area with the 5⁄64-inch drill bit for the arms. Drill a hole through the wider end of each dollhouse-railing arm. To make nailing easier, drill a hole straight down into the pointed end of the egg.

Nail and glue the 3⁄4-inch-diameter wheel to the pointed end of the egg. Glue the open end of the predrilled candle cup to the bottom of the second candle cup. Allow the glue to dry thoroughly.

Apply a coat of gesso to the top candle cup and neck wheel for texture; let the gesso dry. Apply two coats of linen paint to the gesso surfaces, letting the paint dry between coats.

Tear small pieces of the blush patterned tissue paper. Use the sponge brush to apply a thin coat of decoupage medium to the head. Place the paper pieces onto the wet surface one at a time, slightly overlapping the edges. Gently press each piece in place, smoothing to remove bubbles and adhere the edges. Position a piece of the tissue paper at the top of the head to resemble a halo. Decoupage the arms in the same manner. Coat all papered surfaces with the decoupage medium and let dry. Decoupage the lace scrap to the bodice; let dry.

For the skirt, tightly coil one piece of rayon fringe, forming a tassel shape. Hot-glue the coiled end inside the bottom candle cup. Snugly wrap and hot-glue the remaining piece of fringe around the outside of the candle cups, beginning on the bottom cup and ending at the bottom rim of the top cup. Hot-glue the rosebud to the center front waist and hot-glue the candytuft around the waist.

To attach the arms, coil one end of the florist's wire two times around the tip of the needle-nose pliers. Slip the opposite end first through the hole in one arm, then through the predrilled armholes in the candle cup, and finally through the hole in the second arm. Pull the wire so the arms are next to the body, and trim the wire 1⁄4 inch beyond the second arm. Coil the wire end to secure the arms.

For the wings, hot-glue the ends of the feathers to the center back of the angel, positioning three on each side. Hot-glue a small amount of candytuft over the feather ends.

For the hanging loop, knot the narrow cording snugly around the neck so the ends are even. Knot the ends together, forming a loop.

Sweater Stocking

Shown right and on page 18.

YOU WILL NEED

Graph paper
Vintage beaded sweater (pullover or cardigan)
5/8 yard of sage green satin or crepe back satin
Matching sewing thread

INSTRUCTIONS

Enlarge the stocking pattern *pages 90–91* onto graph paper. Cut out the pattern piece. Sew all pieces with right sides together, using 1/2-inch seam allowances unless otherwise noted.

Cut the Fabric

Use the stocking pattern to cut one shape from the vintage sweater for the stocking front, positioning the pattern to utilize the beaded design and construction details such as buttons and pockets. From the remaining portion of the sweater, cut a strip 4×19 inches for the cuff, utilizing the hem or ribbing if desired. (If using ribbing as shown for the taupe color stocking, cut the strip 1½×17 inches.) From sweater fabric, cut a 1½×6-inch strip for the hanging loop.

From the satin fabric, cut one stocking for the stocking back and two for the lining.

Sew the Stocking

Sew the stocking front to the back, leaving the top edge open. Press the seam allowances open as much as possible. Turn the stocking right side out.

Sew the lining front to the back, leaving the top edge open. Trim the seam allowances to 1/4 inch. Zigzag-stitch or overcast the lining seam allowances. Slip the lining inside the stocking with wrong sides facing. Baste together the top edges of the stocking and lining.

For the hanging loop, fold in 1/2 inch on the long edges of the 1½×6-inch strip. Fold the strip in half lengthwise, aligning the folded edges. Machine- or hand-sew the long edges together opposite the fold. Fold the strip in half, forming the loop. Baste the ends to the top inside corner on the heel side of the stocking with the loop inside the stocking.

For the cuff, sew together the short edges of the 19-inch strip, forming a circle. Press the seam allowances open. Slip the cuff inside the stocking with the right side of the cuff facing the stocking lining, aligning the cuff seam with the heel seam and keeping the raw edges even. Sew the cuff to the stocking; press the seam allowances toward the stocking.

Edgestitch around the stocking opening by sewing 1/4 inch from the top of the stocking, through the stocking and seam allowance layers. Turn the cuff to the outside; then fold the hanging loop up toward the cuff.

For the cuff of the taupe stocking, sew together the short edges of the 17-inch strip, forming a circle. Press the seam allowances open. Slip the cuff over the stocking with the right side of the cuff facing the stocking, aligning the cuff seam with the heel seam and keeping the raw edges even. Sew the cuff to the stocking. Fold the cuff up from the stocking and press the seam allowances toward the stocking.

Wool Felt Heart Ornament

Shown at right and on page 16.

YOU WILL NEED

- 5×10-inch piece of ivory wool felt
- Clean terry towel
- Tracing paper
- Seed beads: size 11/0 mauve and size 8/0 pale aqua
- Beading needle
- Ivory sewing thread
- Slubby ivory yarn
- Polyester fiberfill
- 12-inch length of 1-inch-wide lavender bias-cut silk ribbon
- Gold metallic gel pen
- 6-inch length of silver coil bullion

INSTRUCTIONS

To fleece the ivory wool felt, soak it thoroughly in warm water. Blot the excess water on a terry towel and machine-dry for 30 minutes.

Trace the heart pattern *below* onto tracing paper. Cut out the pattern piece. Use the pattern to cut two hearts from the fleeced wool felt. Sew seed beads randomly to one side of one felt heart using ivory sewing thread and a beading needle.

With wrong sides facing, pin the hearts together. Position the slubby yarn around the edges of the layered hearts. Whipstitch the hearts together, catching the yarn in the stitches and leaving a 1-inch opening at the top. Stuff the heart with polyester fiberfill through the opening. Whipstitch the opening closed.

Fold the ribbon in half and finger-crease at the fold. Unfold the ribbon and use the gold gel pen to write "peace on earth" on the right half of the ribbon. Drape the ribbon at an angle across the heart with the center of the ribbon at the upper left edge. Tack the ribbon to the heart at the edges, gathering the ribbon ends together at the lower right edge. Sew seeds beads onto the ribbon on the ornament front.

For the hanging loop, uncoil the silver bullion. Double the bullion layers and sew the ends to the upper edges of the heart.

All designs by Mary Jo Hiney

A GREAT IDEA!

To quickly provide a tree skirt for a themed Earth Angel tree, gather an assortment of linens and laces—table runners, tea towels, place mats, doilies, and so on. Drape them under and around the base of the tree.

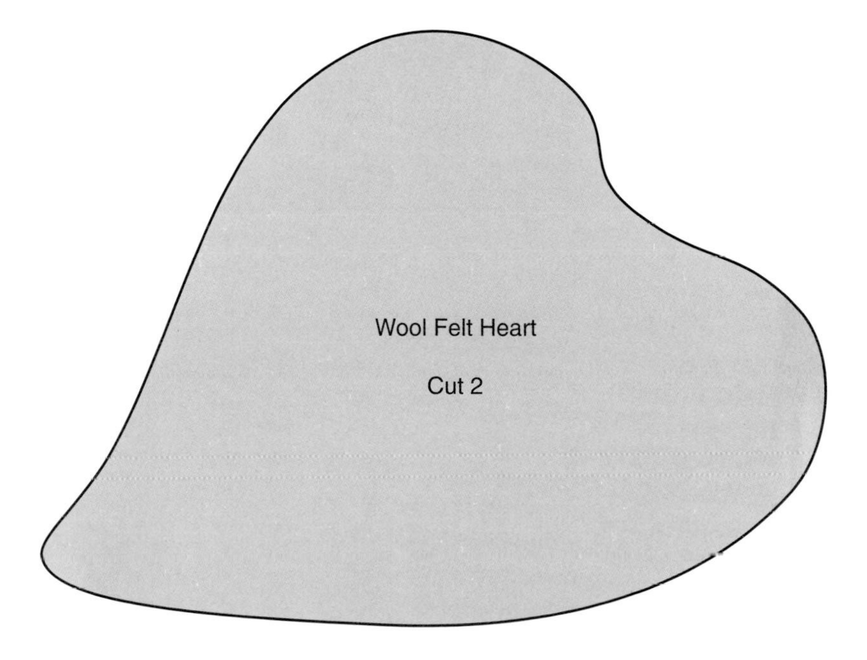

A Way with Wreaths

ONCE A FRONT-DOOR TRADITION of mixed greens, pinecones, and a bow, wreaths have become decorations worthy of personalization. Spruce up an entrance, window, tabletop, or even a gift package with a wreath made of pom-poms, paper, wire, or clay. Or give a wreath of greens a twist by adorning it with gifts that recipients can pluck and enjoy.

For a new mother, enhance a wreath with baby gifts, *above*, or take joy in the beauty of freshly fallen snow with a ring of pom-pom snowmen, *opposite*.

Looking for a way to put pizzazz into your gift wrapping? Wire, a dowel or pencil, and a few beads are all you need. Coils of wire stemming from a circular wire form frame a color-coordinated gift tag to make a diminutive wreath that shimmers as it dangles from a ribbon bow.

If you're uncertain of your flower-arranging skills, try your hand at constructing a wreath that's embellished with paper instead. Snowflake die cuts, chosen in a variety of styles, are decorated with glitter and then pinned to a ribbon-wrapped plastic-foam wreath.

The Christmas ball—long a mainstay of Christmas wreath decorations—gets a new twist when constructed from clay-covered plastic-foam balls. Holly-shaped clay cookie-cutter cutouts applied to the clay-covered balls give texture and dimension to the wreath *opposite*.

Round up a collection of glimmering ornaments and nestle them inside a table wreath, *above*. Wooden star shapes brushed with artificial snow and embellished with small ribbon bows poke between evergreen sprigs decorated with sparkling trims or garland.

Rather than package pretty teas and accessories behind cellophane in a gift basket, create a custom tea-lover's wreath that can be enjoyed first as a decoration, then later as a culinary treat. Ribbon-wrapped teacups hold tea bags for two while handsome tins and a silver infuser complete the ensemble.

Light up the space above a doorway or an area along a fence with a star-shaped wreath cleverly constructed using strips of metal lath. Joined together with carriage bolts and covered with fresh greens and a string of outdoor lights, the decoration can be customized to fit any space.

Snowflake Wreath

Shown below and on page 35.

YOU WILL NEED

- 16-inch plastic-foam wreath form
- 9 yards of 1½-inch-wide white grosgrain ribbon
- 35 to 40 assorted die-cut snowflakes
- Spray adhesive
- Ultra-fine glitters in assorted colors such as celery green, denim blue, blue violet, diamond dust, and turquoise
- Sequin pins

INSTRUCTIONS

Pour one color of glitter onto a paper plate. One at a time, spray one side of six or seven assorted snowflakes with adhesive; then immediately press the glue-coated side of the paper snowflake into the glitter. Continue until the six or seven snowflakes are glittered on one side. Carefully pour the remaining glitter back into the container, and set those snowflakes aside.

Working with groups of six or seven snowflakes at a time, continue to cover one side of the snowflakes with glitter, changing glitter colors after each group has been glittered.

Wrap the wreath form with the ribbon, securing the beginning and end of the ribbon with a pin. Randomly attach the snowflakes to the front of the wreath with sequin pins. Position the pins in the center of some snowflakes, and in the points of others, creating a pleasing array of snowflakes.

Designed by Wendy Musgrave

New Baby Gift Wreath

Shown on page 32.

YOU WILL NEED

- 20-inch fresh mixed green wreath
- Florist's wire
- 5 yards of ½-inch-wide blue-and-white gingham ribbon
- 3½ yards of 1½-inch-wide green wire-edge ribbon
- 2 yards of 1⅜-inch-wide green wire-edge ribbon
- Six baby "gifts" such as: baby bottles, one-piece shirts or t-shirts, baby washcloths, sponge animal, pairs of socks, pair of bootees, two diaper pins, and soft baby rattle
- 3×4-inch rectangle of cream card stock
- ¼-inch hole punch
- Scrapbook embellishment: Baby Boy Outfit #SPJB004 by Jolee's Boutique for EK Success

INSTRUCTIONS

Note: *Although the wreath shown was created in colors fit for a boy, you can purchase gifts and ribbons in colors suited for a girl. The embellishment for the gift tag (shown with a baby boy outfit) can be purchased in a baby girl version; check your favorite crafts or scrapbook store or see Sources on page 158.*

Fold and roll the baby shirts to neatly fit inside the baby bottles. Fasten two pairs of socks together with one diaper pin and fasten a pair of bootees together with another diaper pin. Fold and stack two washcloths with a sponge animal on top. Cut six 28-inch lengths of ½-inch ribbon to attach the baby gifts to the wreath. Evenly position and securely tie each of the gifts to the wreath. Tie the ribbon into a bow at the front of each gift; trim the tails.

To make the gift tag, attach the scrapbook embellishment to the card. Punch a hole in the top center of the

card. Print a congratulatory message at the bottom of the card. Thread a 12-inch length of ½-inch-wide ribbon through the punched hole; knot the ribbon close to the card. Tie the ribbon tails into a loop.

Form a six-loop 10-inch-wide bow; then form a quadruple 6-inch loop bow. Cut a 5-inch length from the ½-inch-wide ribbon; tie the short ribbon around the center of the bow loops. Cut a 1-yard length of florist's wire. Center the bow, and the ribbon loop from the gift tag in the middle of the wire; twist the wire several times to secure the bow. Wire the bow and gift tag to the top center of the wreath.

Designed by Wendy Musgrave

Glitter-Snow Stars Centerpiece Wreath

Shown above and on page 37.

YOU WILL NEED

- 20-inch fresh mixed greenery wreath
- Seven 5-inch wooden star shapes
- Crafts glue
- Sponge brush
- Vintage Mica Snow artificial snow
- Florist's wire
- 2 yards of ½-inch-wide blue organdy ribbon
- 3 yards of gift-wrap trim or ribbon
- Crystal bowl and glass Christmas ornaments

INSTRUCTIONS

Note: *The stars shown have holes drilled through two points (separated by one point). If your stars don't have holes through two points, you can hot-glue the stars to the wreath.*

Thin glue with water; paint thinned glue onto the front and sides of a star. Sprinkle snow over the star; then let dry. Apply glue and snow to the back of the star. Let the glue dry. Repeat for all the stars.

Cut a 4-inch piece of florist's wire; fold the wire in half. Insert the ribbon into the fold of the wire, centering the ribbon. Thread the wire tails through a hole in the point of the star from front to back. Tie the ribbon tails into a knot; then secure the wire on the back of the star. Trim the ribbon tails to the desired lengths. Repeat for all stars.

Cut a 10-inch length of florist's wire, thread one end of the wire into the second hole in a star, and wire the star, points down, into the wreath. Repeat for all stars. String gift-wrap trim or ribbon through the array of stars and greenery. Fill a crystal bowl with glass Christmas ornaments, and place into the center opening of the wreath.

Note: *To hang the wreath, wire or hot-glue the gift-wrap trim and the stars securely to the wreath.*

Designed by staff

Tea Lover's Wreath

Shown on page 38.

YOU WILL NEED

- 20-inch fresh mixed green wreath
- Florist's wire
- 5 yards of ½-inch-wide wine organdy ribbon
- 5 yards of 1⅜-inch-wide wine ribbon
- Six tea "gifts" such as: two teacups or mugs, long-handle tea infuser, canister with loose tea, canister with loose herbal tea, and canister with cookies
- 11 packaged single-serving tea bags
- Cream card stock
- One silver ¼-inch eyelet and eyelet setter
- Pewter teacup charm
- 6-inch length of narrow copper metallic cording
- 20-inch length of ⅛-inch-wide wine ribbon

INSTRUCTIONS

Cut six 30-inch lengths of ½-inch-wide ribbon to attach the tea gifts to the wreath. Evenly position and securely tie each of the gifts to the wreath. Tie the ribbon into a bow at the front of each gift; trim the tails. (When the wreath is finished and hanging up, fill each teacup with five tea bag packages.)

To make the gift tag, cut a rectangle of card stock to fit over the printed part of the label of one of the packaged tea bags. Print a message on the card stock, such as "Tea for two, from me to you!" Use an eyelet setter and eyelet to fasten the card stock message to the front of the tea package. Center and tie the teacup charm on the metallic cording; tie the cording into a loop. Thread the ⅛-inch-wide wine ribbon through the cording loop and the eyelet in the gift tag. Tie the ribbon tails into a loop.

Cut a 1-yard length of 1⅜-inch-wide ribbon for the bow tails. From the remaining length of 1⅜-inch-wide ribbon, form a quadruple 10-inch-wide loop bow; then form a quadruple 6-inch-wide loop bow. Using the ribbon for the bow tails, center and tie the ribbon around the middle of the bow loops. Thread a 1-yard length of florist's wire through the back of the bow and the hanging loop of the gift tag; twist the wire several times to secure. Wire the bow and gift tag to the top center of the wreath.

Designed by Wendy Musgrave

Lighted Outdoor Star Wreath

Shown on page 39.

YOU WILL NEED

- Five lengths of 1-inch-wide metal lath (the length depends on the size of wreath desired—cut all lengths the same)
- Drill
- ¼-inch drill bit
- Five each: ¼-inch bolts, ¼-inch carriage bolts (1¼-inch long), and ¼-inch lock washers
- Florist's wire
- Fresh greenery (or artificial garland and greens for a wreath that can be used year after year)
- Light strands (length to be determined by the wreath size and amount of lights preferred)
- Heavy-gauge wire

INSTRUCTIONS

Center and drill a hole about ¾ inch from each end of each metal lath. Assemble the star shape by putting two metal laths together and securing the ends with a carriage bolt on top, the two laths, a lock washer, and a nut. Referring to the diagram *below*, connect all five laths to form a star shape.

Use lengths of florist's wire to attach greens or artificial garlands and greens to the star. Wire lights to the star; then fill in with more greens as desired.

To hang the wreath, attach heavy-gauge wire to the top three points of the star and wire securely to hooks on the house.

Designed by Wendy Musgrave
Produced by Holly Raibikis

Terra-Cotta and Sage Wreath

Shown opposite and on page 36.

YOU WILL NEED

- 20-inch fresh mixed greenery wreath (or an artificial evergreen wreath)
- Seven 3-inch Styrofoam plastic-foam balls
- DAS Pronto (air-dry) terra-cotta clay
- 4 yards of 1½-inch-wide sage ribbon
- Acrylic paints: buttermilk and copper metallic
- Matte-finish spray varnish
- Holly-leaf cookie cutters, large and small
- Fresh or silk leaves
- Glue gun and hotmelt adhesive
- Crafts glue
- Toothpick

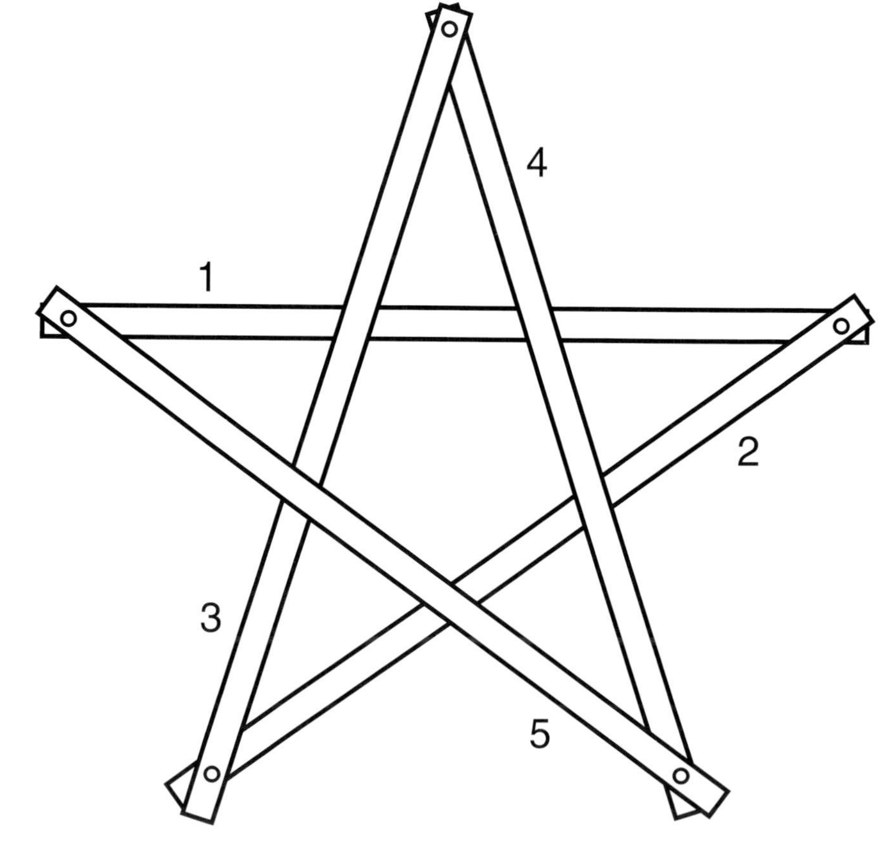

Scissors
Rolling pin
Soft cloth
Waffle-weave place mat or other textured surface

INSTRUCTIONS

Covering the ball with clay

Using a rolling pin, roll out terra-cotta clay approximately ⅛ inch thick. Turn the clay repeatedly to prevent it from sticking to the work surface and the rolling pin.

Spread crafts glue on the ball and then drape the clay over the ball. Press the clay around the ball, using scissors to cut away excess clay. Press out air bubbles as you work around the ball. If an air bubble gets trapped, use a pin to poke a small hole in the clay. Gently roll the ball on a waffle-weave place mat or other surface to give the ball a textured finish.

General decorating instructions

Roll out additional clay approximately ⅛ inch thick, turning repeatedly to prevent the clay from sticking. Cut out leaf shapes as described below for the three different ball designs; then press a fresh or a silk leaf onto the clay leaf to mark the veins. Dip your finger in water and rub the back of the design pieces with your wet finger; gently press the design onto the ball. Use a toothpick to add additional leaf details by accenting the main vein lines in the leaves and poking a hole in the center of the berries.

For a poinsettia-covered ball

Using cookie cutters, cut out small holly leaves. Make a small poinsettia by overlapping five holly leaves in a circle followed by three holly leaves trimmed slightly shorter at one end. Place the three trimmed leaves, trimmed centers together, in the middle of the five leaves. Roll out small balls of clay for berries. Press the berries into the center of the trimmed leaves. Add several more poinsettias to the ball. Use a toothpick to add leaf and berry details.

For a single poinsettia ball

Using cookie cutters, cut out 13 large and five small holly leaves. Attach four large holly leaves vertically around the circumference of the ball (leaving space between each leaf). Attach the next four leaves ½ inch higher, and between the previous four leaves, overlapping them. Trim the remaining large leaves by ½ inch and lay them on top of the previous leaves, trimmed centers together. Attach the final five small holly leaves in the center of the previous trimmed leaves. Roll out multiple small balls of clay for berries. Press the berries into the center of the last five leaves. Use a toothpick to add leaf and berry details.

Holly-leaf vine covered ball

Using cookie cutters, cut out holly leaf shapes. Randomly place leaves over the ball. Make stems by rolling out thin clay ropes and trailing them between the leaves. Roll out multiple small balls of clay for berries. Use a toothpick to add leaf and berry details.

Finishing the ball ornaments

Let the clay-covered balls dry. Thin buttermilk paint with water and cover the ball with a coat of thinned paint. Using a soft cloth, immediately wipe away excess paint, leaving paint in the crevices. Dip your finger into the copper paint, and gently rub across the tops of all design elements on the balls, highlighting the leaves, stems, and berries. Repeat as necessary. Let the paint dry. Spray the balls with two coats of matte-finish varnish, allowing the varnish to dry after each coat.

Assembling the Wreath

Tie a four-loop bow with 1½ yards of sage ribbon. Wrap the wreath with the remaining sage ribbon, making sure there are evenly spaced open areas to attach the seven decorated balls. If using a fresh wreath, trim away spots in the open areas between the ribbon wraps, or fluff an artificial wreath, bending the evergreen sprays until the wreath looks full. Hot-glue or wire the bow in place at the top of the wreath. Glue the balls into the open areas between the ribbon wraps encircling the wreath.

Designed by Lorine Mason

Snowmen Wreath

Shown right and on page 33.

YOU WILL NEED

- 12-inch wire wreath frame
- Flat white interior/exterior spray paint (we used Krylon)
- 3 skeins (137 yards each) of white 100-percent polyester yarn (we used Sirdar Snowflake)
- Jumbo pom-pom maker
- Four toothpicks
- Orange acrylic paint
- Paintbrush
- Tracing paper
- Felt: black, turquoise, light turquoise, and lime
- Small amount of polyester fiberfill
- Eight white iris chenille stems
- 5-millimeter black pom-poms
- Crafts glue
- Silver color fine-gauge wire
- Glue gun and hotmelt adhesive
- Spray adhesive
- Vintage Mica Snow artificial snow

INSTRUCTIONS

Spray-paint the wreath frame white. Allow the paint to dry; then spray-paint again. Let the paint dry.

Using the largest size of pom-pom maker (our pom-poms are about 4-inches in diameter), make three pom-poms for each of the four snowmen. Use a 20-inch length of wire to wrap the center of each pom-pom; then wire the pom-poms to the front of the wreath frame. Trim every third pom-pom slightly smaller (to about $3\frac{1}{2}$ inches) for heads.

Paint the toothpicks orange; let them dry. Hot-glue one end of each toothpick nose into the middle of a pom-pom head. Use crafts glue to attach two black pom-pom eyes and five pom-poms for the mouth to each head; let the glue dry.

For the hat, trace the hat pattern, *below*. Cut out the pattern. For each hat, cut two hat shapes from the black felt. Hot-glue the two hat shapes together along three sides, leaving the bottom open. Lightly stuff the hat with fiberfill. Cut a 12-inch length of wire; fold the wire in half. Insert the fold of the wire into the hat opening; glue the bottom of the hat shut. Cut a $\frac{1}{4}\times1\frac{3}{4}$-inch strip from the turquoise or light turquoise felt for the hatband. Hot-glue the band to the top of the hat. Make three more hats. Wire a hat to the top of each head, threading both wires through the pom-pom head near the top. Tilt the hat right or left, alternating directions for each snowman.

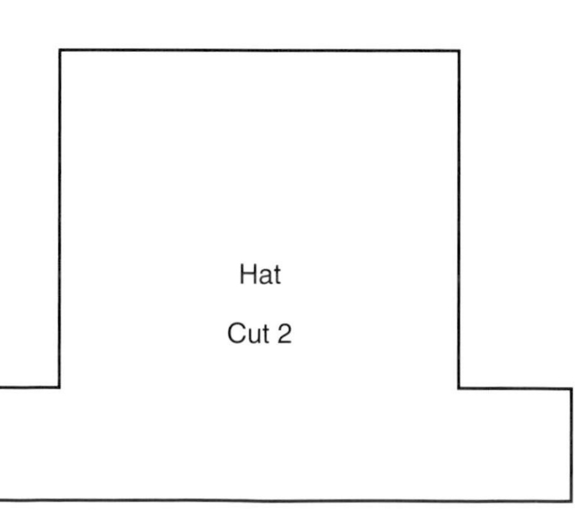

For the scarf, cut two 1-inch-wide strips from the turquoise or light turquoise felt; one 7-inches long, the other 5-inches long. Snip a $\frac{1}{2}$-inch fringe at each end of the 7-inch strip. Fold the strip in half, slightly askew, then decorate the ends of the folded strip (top side only) with pieces of contrasting felt. Refer to the photo *above* for decorating ideas. Cut a

10-inch length of wire; center and hot-glue the wire to the back of the 5-inch strip of felt. Let the glue cool; then flip the felt over, and glue the folded end of the decorated scarf piece, slightly off-center on the right side of the wired-scarf strip. Attach the scarf to the "neck" just below the head. Repeat for three more scarves, making each one slightly different from the others.

To make each arm, bend a chenille stem in half; then twist the halves together, starting about 1¼ inches below the bend. Push the bend down to meet at the twist, making a V-shape for the hand. Wire and hot-glue the ends of the chenille stem to the frame behind the back of the body pom-pom. Repeat for the second arm. Make and attach two arms to each snowman.

Lightly spray adhesive over the front of the wreath. Sprinkle the snow over the adhesive; shake off the excess. Attach a wire hanger to the back of the wreath frame.

Designed by Wendy Musgrave

Wire Gift-Tag Wreath

Shown below and on page 34.

YOU WILL NEED

- 18-gauge silver-colored wire
- 18-gauge blue-colored wire
- 24-gauge green-colored wire
- Assorted glass beads in green, blue, and silver (with holes large enough to fit onto the coated wire)
- 12-inch length of ⅛-inch dowel rod
- 12-inch length of ¼-inch dowel rod
- E6000 adhesive
- Coordinating gift wrap
- Wide and narrow ribbon
- Card stock for a gift tag
- Silver cording

INSTRUCTIONS

Note: *The designer used plastic-coated wire, but uncoated colored wire is readily available at crafts stores.*

Form a 3-inch-diameter ring of two or three coils of silver wire; secure the ring of wire by wrapping additional wire around the ring. Cut 60 or more 4-to-7-inch lengths of wire from all three colors of wire. Wrap a length of the cut wire around a dowel rod, leaving nearly 1 inch straight at one end. Remove the coiled wire from the dowel, and pull on the wire to open the coils slightly. On the coiled end of some of the wires, thread a bead onto the curled end; then secure each bead by bending the end of the wire over. After all the wire lengths have been coiled on either the ⅛-inch dowel rod or the ¼-inch dowel rod, bend the straight end of a coiled wire around the silver ring. Add all the coils to the ring in the same manner.

Form a single 3-inch ring from the green wire, but do not close the ring. Thread assorted beads on the wire to cover the ring; twist the wire ends together to secure the ring. Hide the wire twist on the back of the ring. Use a small amount of E6000 adhesive to secure the beaded ring to the wire-and-coil ring. Let the adhesive dry.

Wrap a gift package in coordinating paper. Cut and wrap the box once with two ribbons, one wide and one narrow, leaving two long ribbon tails. Allow the ribbon tails to hang straight down the front of the gift box; thread the ribbons through the wire wreath. Fold the ends of the ribbons over to hold the wreath. Wrap the combined ribbons with a single coil of wire to securely hold the wreath in place. Make a paper tag with the gift recipient's name on it, and use silver cording to hang the gift tag from the center of the wreath. Make a bow with wide ribbon and attach the bow to the ribbons at the top of the gift box.

Designed by Wendy Musgrave

Holidays
Merry
Christmas

Red-and-White Whimsy

PERHAPS INSPIRED BY SANTA'S fur-trimmed suit or the swirls of a peppermint candy, red-and-white never seems to lose its holiday flair.

To keep your holiday scheme fresh yet traditional, create a tree that combines crisp whites with deep reds in a variety of textures and patterns. On the tree *opposite*, gingham-ribbon tassels twirl beside ring-tag swags and fuzzy-roofed houses, *above*. Plush felt strawberries, an icy-looking mantel drape, and a vintage postcard wreath add soft touches to the mix.

Enliven an artificial wreath by tucking favorite Christmas cards in between the branches, *above*. Choose cards with coordinating color schemes or similar themes, such as the Santas shown. Where some see a simple metal-rimmed tag, a plain demitasse cup, an ordinary Christmas ball, or a typical chandelier crystal, creative minds see spectacular Christmas ornaments. Peppermint-striped letter stickers spell out holiday messages on ring tags, a ring of beads encircles a painted Christmas ball, painted swirls and dots adorn a glass teardrop crystal, and trims and a star decorate a plain demitasse cup, *opposite*.

GREETINGS

GREETIN

Old World meets fun and funky when this nostalgic Santa Claus doll is paired up with a shaggy-cuffed red-and-white stocking, *opposite*. Facial details from paint and the turned-up felt beard make Santa's expression irresistible. White satin cording whip-stitched with red thread creates a candy-canelike motif.

Red-and-white means everything bright on ornaments such as salvaged holiday stamps made into framed artwork that recall happy holiday memories, *above*. Plump strawberries, miniature tiered cakes stands, and tassels with swirls of candy-striped ribbon will start mouths watering.

Santa Time Clock Ornament

Shown below and on page 46.

YOU WILL NEED

- $2\frac{1}{4}$-inch-diameter round box, base only
- Drill
- Drill bits, $\frac{5}{64}$-inch and $\frac{7}{32}$-inch
- Sandpaper
- Clean cloth
- Two $\frac{7}{8}$-inch wooden apples
- Wood glue
- Masking tape
- Two $1\frac{3}{8}$-inch axle pegs
- Hammer
- Acrylic paints, red and white
- Paintbrushes
- White pearl glitter
- Red paint pen
- White embroidery floss
- Crafts glue
- Santa image
- Black fine-tip Pigma pen

INSTRUCTIONS

Use a pencil to make a small T centered on one side of the box base for the center top of the clock. Make a small B on the opposite side for the center bottom. Make a mark 1 inch on each side of the T and B. Use the $\frac{5}{64}$-inch drill bit to make a hole through the side of the base at the T for the hanging loop. Use the $\frac{7}{32}$-inch drill bit to make a hole through the marks on either side of the B for the legs. Lightly sand the box and wipe away the sanding dust with a clean cloth.

Use wood glue to glue the apples, tops down, on the box base at the marks on either side of the T. Tape the apples in place with masking tape. When the glue is dry, remove the tape. For the legs, hammer the axle pegs into the holes at the bottom of the clock.

Apply two coats of red paint to all outside surfaces of the clock except the front rim, letting the paint dry between coats. While the second coat is still wet, sprinkle glitter over the wet paint; let dry. Apply two coats of white to the inside surfaces of the clock. Immediately after applying the second white coat, sprinkle a generous amount of glitter onto the wet paint inside the clock. When the paint has dried, paint the front rim with two coats of white. When the rim is dry, use the paint pen to draw stripes on the front rim.

For the hanging loop, cut a 9-inch length of floss. Fold the floss in half, forming a loop; knot the ends together. Working from inside the clock, insert the folded end of the loop through the center top hole. Pull the loop until the knot rests against the inside of the clock; glue in place.

Trim the Santa image into a circle to fit inside the clock. Draw the clock face on the circle with the black pen. Glue the circle inside the clock.

Chenille Icicle Ornament

Shown above right and on page 46.

YOU WILL NEED

- 12-inch length of silver metallic chenille stem
- 7-inch length of florist's wire

INSTRUCTIONS

Fold over $\frac{1}{2}$ inch at one end of the chenille stem, forming a loop. Wrap the stem part below the loop around your index finger. Pull down on the wraps, loosening the coil as desired. Thread the florist's wire through the loop to hang the ornament.

Cake Plate Ornament

Shown above left and on page 51.

YOU WILL NEED

- 1-inch, $1\frac{1}{2}$-inch, and $1\frac{3}{4}$-inch wooden hearts
- Drill
- $\frac{5}{64}$-inch drill bits,
- $3\frac{1}{2}$-inch length of wooden skewer
- White acrylic paint
- Paintbrush
- Glue gun and hotmelt adhesive
- Two 1-inch-diameter Styrofoam plastic-foam balls
- 12-inch length of red metallic chenille
- E6000 adhesive

Four bouquets of tiny red roses
Red stamens
Four 6-millimeter silver beads
Wire cutters

INSTRUCTIONS

Drill a hole at the center of each heart. Apply two coats of white paint to all surfaces of the hearts and skewer, letting the paint dry between coats.

Glue one end of the skewer into the hole in the big heart so that skewer is flush with the bottom. Slip the medium heart on the skewer and glue in place 1½ inches above the bottom heart. Slip the small heart on the skewer and glue in place 3 inches above the bottom heart.

Cut the plastic-foam balls into quarters. Glue two quarters to the center top of each heart around the skewer, creating a mound. Cut a 2½-inch length of red chenille; bend the chenille in half, forming a loop. Twist the ends together. Insert and glue the chenille ends into the mound on the small heart.

Cut the rose stems to measure ⅜ inch. Insert and glue the rose stems into the plastic-foam mounds on each heart, forming tiny flower arrangements. Cut red stamen stems to measure ⅜ inch. Insert and glue stamens among the roses.

Cut two 3-inch lengths of chenille for the legs and set aside. Cut the remaining chenille into 1-inch lengths. Tightly curl one end of each piece of chenille. Insert and glue the straight end of the chenille curls into the flower arrangements.

Crisscross the two 3-inch lengths of chenille and twist them together at the center. Slip a silver bead onto each leg. Curl ends to secure beads in place. Glue legs to the bottom of the large heart with E6000 adhesive.

Christmas Stamp Ornament

Shown at right and on page 51.

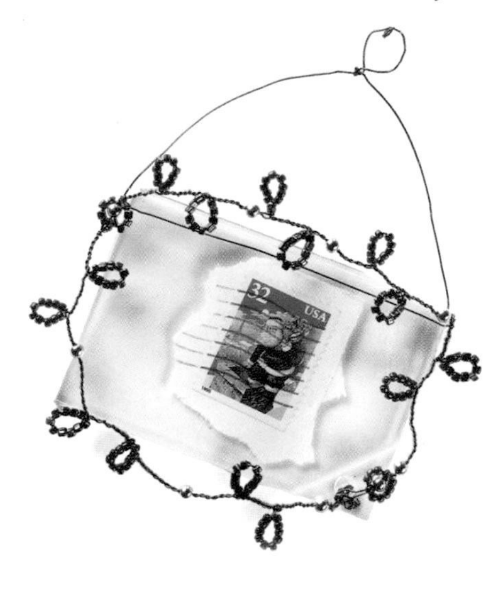

YOU WILL NEED

26-gauge red wire
Wire cutters
Two shades of red seed beads
Nine 3-millimeter silver beads
2×3-inch clear plastic fold-over frame
Recycled Christmas postage stamp

INSTRUCTIONS

Cut a 54-inch length of red wire for the beaded garland. Bend the wire in half, forming a loop at one end. Beginning at the loop end, twist the wires together for ½ inch. Separate the wires below the twisted area, and slide 10 seed beads of the same shade onto the left wire snug against the twisted area. Bend the beaded wire to form a small loop, and twist the bottom of the loop to secure. Twist the two wires together below the loop for ½ inch. Slide 10 seed beads of the second shade on the right wire and bend to form the second loop.

Twist the two wires together for ½ inch and slide a silver bead onto the twisted area. Repeat the steps to make alternating loops of the two bead shades, twisting the wires together for ½ inch after each loop and adding a silver bead after every two loops for the length of the wire.

For the hanging loop, cut an 11-inch length of wire. Center the wire in the fold of the frame. Shape the beaded garland around the front edges of the frame, twisting the ends together.

To attach the garland, wrap an end of the hanging loop wire around each top corner of the garland. Twist the hanging loop wires together about 1 ½ inches above the top center of the frame, and then twist the wire ends together. Slip and center the stamp in the frame.

Strawberry Ornament

Shown on page 51.

YOU WILL NEED

Tracing paper
3×6-inch piece of red felt
Ivory seed beads
Beading needle
Red cotton embroidery floss
Off-white rayon embroidery floss
Embroidery needle
Polyester fiberfill
Five small ivory velvet leaves
Glue gun and hotmelt adhesive
Vintage ladybug pin or small red bells

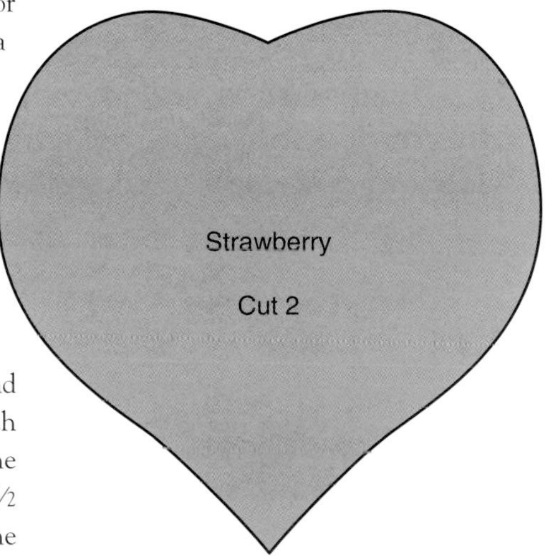

INSTRUCTIONS

Trace the pattern on *page 13* onto tracing paper. Cut out the pattern piece. Using the pattern, cut two pieces from the red felt for the ornament front and back. Randomly sew ivory seed beads on one side of each felt piece with red embroidery floss and the beading needle.

With wrong sides facing, use two plies of off-white rayon floss to whipstitch the edges of the strawberry front and back together, leaving a 1-inch opening along the top. Stuff the strawberry with polyester fiberfill and whipstitch the opening closed.

For the hanging loop, use an embroidery needle to thread a 9-inch length of red floss through the top center of the ornament; knot the ends of the floss together.

Hot-glue the off-white leaves to the top front and back of the strawberry. Hot-glue the ladybug or sew the bells to the center top of the ornament.

Eggcup Lady Ornament

Shown below and on page 46.

YOU WILL NEED

- Small wooden eggcup
- Acrylic paints: brown, flesh tone of your choice, red, and white
- Paintbrushes
- Black fine-tip Pigma pen
- Plastic foam ball to fit in cup
- Foam glue
- 3-inch length of red rhinestone trim
- E6000 adhesive
- 2×5-inch piece of fake fur
- Sewing threads, red and ivory
- 1×22-inch strip of red felt
- 1¼-inch-diameter circle template
- Seven ivory velvet leaves
- 9-inch length of red embroidery floss
- Glue gun and hotmelt adhesive

INSTRUCTIONS

Apply two coats of flesh tone paint to the outside surfaces of the eggcup, letting the paint dry between coats. Referring to the photograph *below left*, use a pencil to draw facial features lightly on the front of the cup. Paint the eyes white, add a brown circle for the irises, and a tiny white highlight dot. Use red for the lips. Mix a little red with white. Use this mixture for the cheeks. Use the black pen to outline the eyes and lips and to draw the eyebrows, nose, and mouth lines.

Cut the plastic-foam ball in half. Use foam glue to glue one half, cut side up, inside the eggcup. For the necklace, wrap rhinestone trim around the neck and glue the ends to the center back with E6000 adhesive. For the shawl, wrap the fake fur around the base and glue in place. Sew running stitches along the bottom edge of the fur. Pull the thread to gather the fur around the bottom of the eggcup; knot to secure.

To scallop the felt, use the circle template to trace half-circles along one long edge of the 1×22-inch felt strip; cut on the traced lines. Thread a needle and knot the ends together. Sew running stitches ⅛ inch from the straight long edge of the felt strip. Pull the thread, gathering the felt to measure 8½ inches. Knot the thread, but do not cut it. Tightly roll the first two scallops for the flower center and sew at the bottom with the uncut thread to secure. Continue to wrap the gathered felt around the center of the flower, sewing the felt at the bottom.

For the hanging loop, fold the red floss in half, forming a loop; knot the ends together. Insert the folded end of the loop through a needle and pull the loop up through the center of the flower until the knot rests against the bottom of the flower.

Glue the wide end of the leaves on the plastic foam, draping the leaves over the top edge of the eggcup to frame the face. Glue the flower onto the plastic foam.

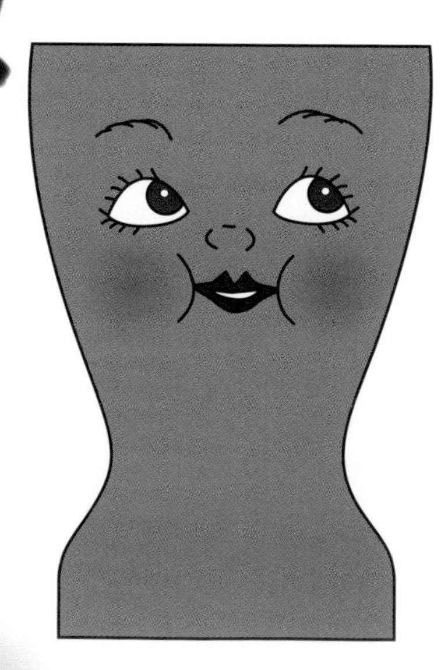

Painted Crystal Ornament

Shown on page 49.

YOU WILL NEED

Glass chandelier crystal
Pēbēo Vitrea 160 glass paint: Pepper Red
Paintbrush
18-inch length of 3/8-inch-wide red gingham ribbon

INSTRUCTIONS

Wash the crystal in warm soapy water or clean with rubbing alcohol. Use Pepper Red to paint a design on the crystal as desired. (We painted stripes dots, and squiggles on the ornaments shown.) Let the paint dry for 24 hours. To make the paint permanent, bake the painted crystal, following the paint manufacturer's instructions.

For the hanging loop, insert the ribbon through the metal hook at the top of the crystal. Fold the ribbon in half, forming a loop. Knot the ribbon to the hook 3 inches from the fold; tie the ends in a bow.

Ribbon Tassel Ornament

Shown at left and on page 51.

YOU WILL NEED

1 1/4-inch-tall wooden candle cup
Acrylic paints, red and white
Paintbrushes
White pearl glitter
6 1/2 yards of 3/8-inch-wide red gingham ribbon
White sewing thread and needle
Three 1/2-inch red glass balls
1 yard of white narrow string
9-inch length of 3/16-inch-wide red velvet ribbon
Crafts glue

INSTRUCTIONS

Apply two coats of white paint to all surfaces of the candle cup, letting the paint dry between coats. Use red to paint the bottom and the rim of the cup and to add angled stripes. Immediately pour a small amount of glitter onto the wet paint. Set the cup aside to dry.

Cut twenty-eight 8 1/2-inch lengths of gingham ribbon. Fold one ribbon length in half. Thread the needle and knot the ends together. Sew small running stitches through both ribbon layers about 1/4 inch from the cut ends. Using the same thread, repeat with the remaining ribbon lengths, making a chain of ribbon loops. Pull the thread as tightly as possible to gather the ribbon loops. Secure thread but do not cut it.

Cut three 12-inch lengths of string. Center a glass ball on each string. Fold each string length in half and knot the ends together. Sew the knotted end of the strung balls to the last ribbon loop. Tightly roll the gathered ends of the ribbon loops, using the excess gathering thread, sew the roll together to form a ribbon tassel with dangling glass balls at the center.

For the hanging loop, fold the velvet ribbon in half, forming a loop; knot together the ribbon ends. Working from inside the candle cup, insert the folded end of the velvet ribbon through the hole. Pull the ribbon so the knot rests against the inside of the cup; glue the knot in place. Glue the ribbon tassel in the cup.

Demitasse Topiary Ornament

Shown on pages 49 and 57.

YOU WILL NEED

White demitasse cup
1/4 yard each of two narrow red trims
E6000 adhesive
Small piece of plastic foam
5-inch length of 3/16-inch-diameter wooden dowel
White acrylic paint
Paintbrush
1/3 yard of red rattail cord
Tracing paper
3×6-inch piece of red felt
Four 1-inch-diameter plastic snowflakes
Off-white rayon embroidery floss
Polyester fiberfill
Crafts glue
Embroidery needle

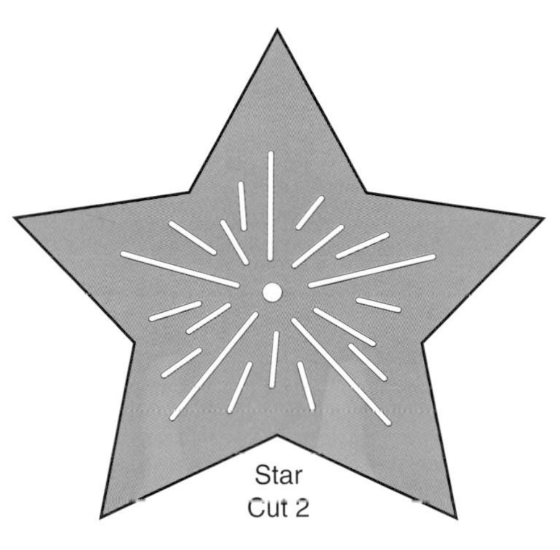

INSTRUCTIONS

Glue the trims to the top and bottom edges of the cup with E6000 adhesive. Let the adhesive dry. Cut the plastic foam to fit into the cup ½ inch below the top edge. Glue the plastic foam inside the cup.

Apply two coats of white paint to the dowel, letting the paint dry between coats. Wrap the rattail cord to spiral around the dowel, gluing the ends at the top and bottom.

Trace the pattern on *page 55* onto tracing paper. Cut out the pattern piece. Using the pattern, cut two pieces from the red felt for the star front and back. Use two plies of off-white rayon floss to straight-stitch a star on the center front of one felt star.

With wrong sides facing, use two plies of off-white floss to whip-stitch the edges of the star front and back together, leaving a 1-inch opening at the center bottom. Stuff the star with polyester fiberfill. Insert and glue one end of the dowel in the opening. Whipstitch the opening closed.

Insert and glue the remaining end of the dowel into the center of the plastic foam. Glue snowflakes to cover the plastic foam.

House Ornament

Shown below and on page 47.

YOU WILL NEED

- Tracing paper
- One sheet of red velvet paper
- 4×8-inch piece of crescent board
- Scoring tool
- Glue gun and hotmelt adhesive
- Scraps of white watercolor paper
- Deckle-edge scissors
- Red fine-tip marking pen
- Two 1-inch plastic candy canes
- Crafts glue
- 1½-inch square of off-white wool felt
- Pinking shears
- 1½×5-inch piece of ivory fake fur
- 9-inch length of red embroidery floss
- 1½×5-inch piece of ivory card stock
- Six 3-millimeter silver beads
- Two 6-millimeter silver beads
- Two red seed beads

INSTRUCTIONS

Trace the patterns on *page 58* onto tracing paper. Cut out the pattern pieces. Use the house pattern to cut one house from the red velvet paper. From the crescent board, use the patterns to cut reinforcement pieces as follows: two front/back pieces, two sides, one base, two windows, and one door.

Score the red velvet house on the dashed lines. Fold on the scored lines. Hot-glue the crescent board pieces, excluding the windows and door, to the corresponding locations on the wrong side of the velvet house.

Attach scraps of watercolor paper to one side of the door and windows with crafts glue. Trim the excess watercolor paper close with the deckle-edge scissors. Use the red marker to add the details to the door and windows. Hot-glue the door and windows to the house front. Use crafts glue to glue the candy canes to the windows. Let the glue dry.

Fold the house along the previously folded lines; hot-glue at the side and bottom edges. Trim the edges of the felt square with a pinking shears. Center and glue the felt to the bottom of the house.

For the hanging loop, use a needle to thread a 9-inch length of red floss through the center of the fake fur; knot the ends of the floss together on the wrong side of the fur. Hot-glue the fur to the ivory card stock for the roof. For a beaded dangle, thread a needle; knot one end. Beginning on the fur side, bring the needle through the roof about ¼ inch from the center of a short edge. Thread on two small silver beads, one large silver bead, one small silver bead, and one seed bead. Return the needle through all but the seed bead and knot on the fur side of the roof. Repeat for the opposite edge of the roof. Fold the roof in half and hot-glue to the house, slightly curving up the ends.

Wishes Swag Ornament

Shown opposite and on page 49.

YOU WILL NEED

- 1½-inch metal-rimmed tags, one for each letter
- 1¼-inch-high candy cane sticker letters
- ⅛-inch-wide red-and-white trim
- Two ¾-inch-diameter red bells
- White sewing thread
- Sewing needle
- Disappearing ink pen

INSTRUCTIONS

Place a sticker on the front and back of each tag to spell the desired word.

Beginning 4 inches from one end of the trim, use the disappearing ink pen to mark 1¾-inch intervals along the length of the trim for each letter. Cut the trim 4 inches beyond the last mark.

Tie the tags onto the trim at each mark. Tie a bell onto the trim 1¾ inches from the first and last letters. Fold the trim ends to form a small loop at each end. Sew the ends to the trim near each bell.

Beaded Chenille Wreath

Shown above left and on page 49.

YOU WILL NEED

- 1-inch ivory frosted glass bulb
- Red paint pen
- 12-inch length of silver metallic chenille stem
- ½-inch red glass bulb
- Four 6-millimeter red round glass beads
- Six 6-millimeter silver round beads

INSTRUCTIONS

Use the paint pen to add designs to the ivory frosted glass bulb and set aside to dry. Slide the red glass bulb onto the center of the chenille stem.

Thread three silver and two red beads onto each side of the stem, alternating the beads and spacing them about ⅜ inch apart. Bend the beaded stem into a circle and slip both ends through the hanger of the ivory bulb. Twist the stem around the hanger, securing the circle shape. Form a small loop with the remaining stem and twist the ends together. Trim the stem if necessary.

Lidded Jar Ornament

Shown at right. and on page 46.

YOU WILL NEED

- 1½x3½-inch glass jar with attached clamp-on glass lid
- Laser-cut stickers: stripes and lace edging designs
- Sheer Christmas sticker for jar lid
- Red hot candies or red sugar, enough to fill jar
- 9-inch length of ⅛-inch-wide red satin ribbon
- Florist's wire

INSTRUCTIONS

Clean the jar and lid with soapy water, rinse well, and allow the glass to dry. Cut and apply the sticker stripes vertically to the jar sides. Apply the lace-edging sticker around the bottom edge of the jar and a sheer sticker to the jar lid.

Fill the jar with red hot candies or red sugar. Tie the ribbon into a bow on the metal clamp at the front of the jar. Hang the jar securely from the tree using florist's wire.

Red Felt Stocking

Shown on page 50.

YOU WILL NEED

- Graph paper
- ⅓ yard of red felt
- ⅛ yard of long-haired red imitation fur
- 2 yards of white rattail cording
- Straight pins
- Red embroidery floss
- Embroidery needle
- Five small white bells
- One large white bell

INSTRUCTIONS

Enlarge the stocking pattern on *pages 90-91* onto graph paper. Cut out the pattern piece.

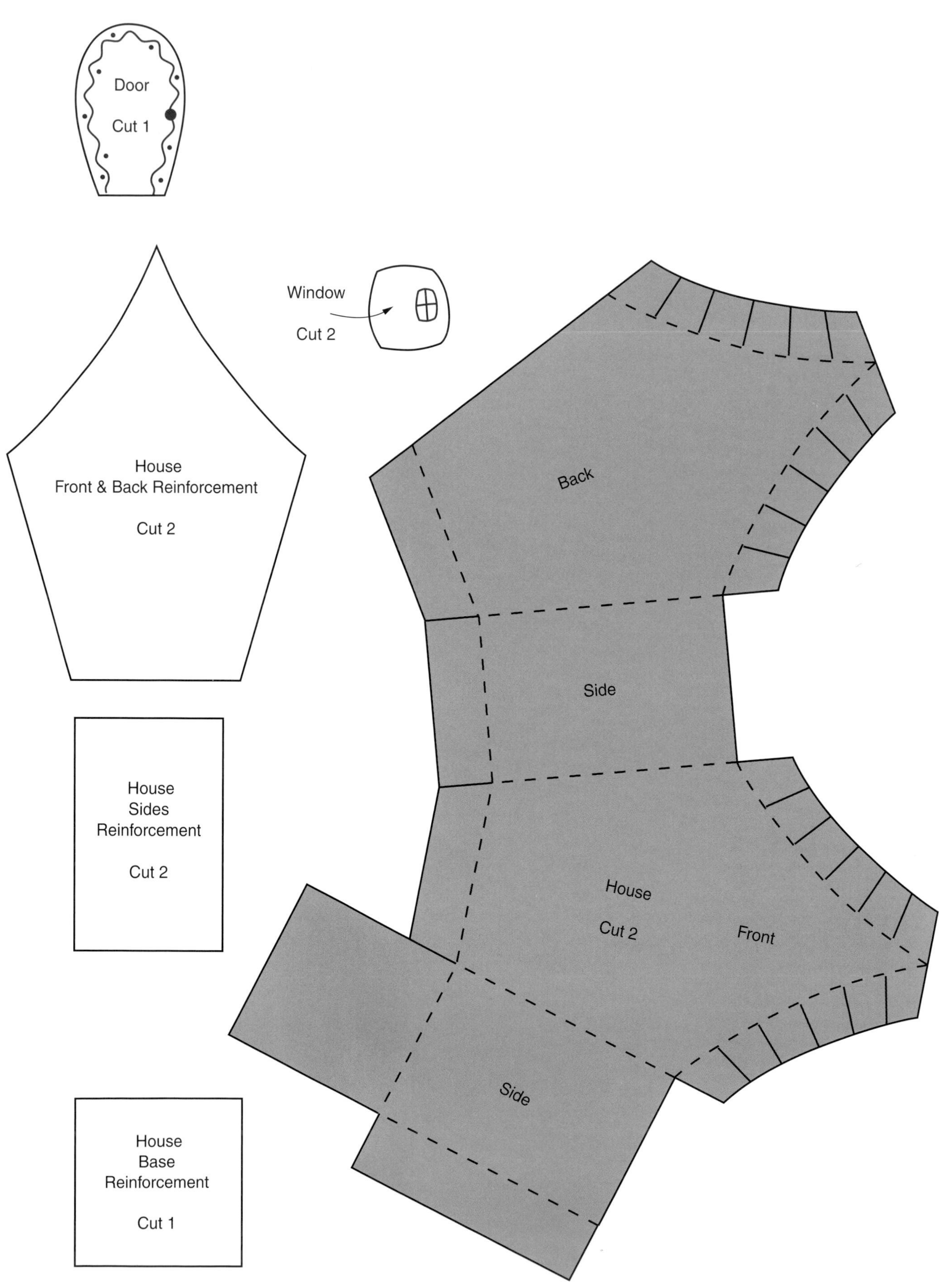

Door
Cut 1
Window
Cut 2
House
Front & Back Reinforcement
Cut 2
House
Sides
Reinforcement
Cut 2
House
Base
Reinforcement
Cut 1
Back
Side
House
Cut 2
Front
Side

Note: *Sew all pieces with right sides together, using ¼-inch seam allowances unless otherwise noted.*

Cut the Fabric

From the red felt, cut two stockings and one 1×5-inch hanging strip. From the imitation fur, cut a 3½×19-inch strip for the cuff.

Sew the Stocking

Place one felt stocking on a flat surface. Beginning and ending at an outer edge, randomly swirl the cording onto the stocking front. When pleased with the design, anchor the cording with straight pins. Use two plies of floss to whipstitch cording in place.

Sew the stocking front to the back, leaving the top edge open. Clip the curves. Press the seam allowances open. Turn the stocking right side out.

For the hanging loop, fold the 1×5-inch strip in half, aligning the long edges. Sew the long edges together. Fold the strip in half, forming a loop. Baste the ends to the inside top corner on the heel edge of the stocking with the loop inside the stocking.

For the cuff, sew the short edges together, pushing the fur away from the seam while sewing. Finger-press the seam allowances open. Slip the cuff inside the stocking with the right side of the cuff facing the wrong side of the stocking and aligning the cuff seam with the center front seam of the stocking.

Sew the top edges together with a ½-inch seam allowance. Pull the cuff away from the stocking and press the seam allowances toward the stocking. Edgestitch around the stocking opening by sewing ¼ inch from the top of the stocking, through the stocking and seam allowance layers. Turn the cuff to the outside.

Sew the small bells to the foot of the stocking, spacing them 1½ inches apart. Sew the large bell to the center bottom of the cuff front.

Christmas Card Wreath

Shown on page 48.

YOU WILL NEED

- 24-inch artificial evergreen wreath
- Old Christmas cards and die cuts in assorted sizes
- Variety of decorative-edge scissors
- Florist's wire
- Wire cutters
- Twelve 1-inch cream glass bulbs
- Spray adhesive
- Silver glitter
- Three vintage berry clusters
- Silver, red, and gold metallic chenille stems
- 24 red berry stamens
- 2½ yards of 1-inch-wide red velvet ribbon
- Two chandelier prisms
- 1 yard of ivory embroidery floss

INSTRUCTIONS

Arrange the cards and die cuts on the wreath. When pleased with the arrangement, use the decorative-edge scissors to trim the edges of the cards. Use 8-inch lengths of florist's wire to wire the cards and die cuts in place, concealing the wire in the greenery.

Spray the glass bulbs with adhesive. Immediately sprinkle silver glitter onto the adhesive. When dry, wire the bulbs around the wreath. Position the berry clusters on the wreath; secure with wire.

Wrap a piece of silver, red, or gold chenille stem around each berry stamen, bringing the stem over the top center of the berry. Use wire to wrap the stamens together in pairs. Wire the stamen pairs around the wreath, filling in any open spaces.

Drape the ribbon around the wreath, positioning the tails at the upper left side and wiring it in place. Tie a bow with the tails. Cut the floss in half. Thread a chandelier prism to the center of each length of floss; knot the ends together. Tie the crystal prisms onto the wreath.

Icicle Mantel Cloth

Shown on page 48.

Note: *The finished mantel cloth is 72 inches long. Adjust the felt yardage as needed for your mantel.*

YOU WILL NEED

- 2 yards of 36-inch-wide off-white wool felt
- Matching sewing thread
- Tracing paper
- Gray pencil

INSTRUCTIONS

Fold the felt in half, aligning the long edges; press. Sew the layers together ¼ inch from the fold. Find the width of your mantel. Measuring from the fold, use straight pins to mark that width along the length of the felt.

Trace the icicle pattern on *pages 60–61*, connecting the two halves of the pattern; cut out. Position the pattern on one end of the felt with the straight edge of the pattern along the pin line. Use a gray pencil to trace the bottom edges of the icicles onto the felt. Reposition the pattern on the felt to draw icicles across the entire length of the felt.

Pin the felt layers together inside the traced lines. Sew ⅛ inch inside the traced lines and continue the stitching on the side edges to the top fold. Cut away the excess felt along the drawn lines.

Santa Doll

Shown on pages 50 and 64.

YOU WILL NEED

- Tracing paper
- 3/8 yard of muslin fabric
- 1/4 yard of off-white silk noil fabric
- 1/3 yard of red-and-ivory plaid fabric
- 1/8 yard of short-haired ivory imitation fur
- 1 square of red felt
- 1/8 yard of ivory wool felt
- 1/2 yard of red-and-white double-sided jacquard fabric
- 1/8 yard of long-haired red imitation fur
- Matching sewing threads
- Polyester fiberfill
- Plastic pellets
- One 3-inch-diameter wooden circle or eight 3-inch-diameter crescent board circles
- Crafts glue
- Glue gun and hotmelt adhesive
- Acrylic paints: flesh tone of your choice, white, brown, and red
- Paintbrushes
- Black fine-tip Pigma pen
- 5/8 yard of 3/8-inch-wide red-and-white ribbon
- 1/2 yard of 1-inch-wide red velvet ribbon
- 1-inch silver belt buckle
- Three small red bells
- Four chenille stems
- One 3 1/2-inch–diameter wooden circle or four 3 1/2-inch-diameter crescent board circles
- Artificial berry evergreen spray

INSTRUCTIONS

Trace the pattern pieces on *pages 62–63 and 65–67*. Cut out the pattern pieces. **Note:** *Sew all pieces with right sides together using 1/4-inch seam allowances, unless otherwise noted.*

Icicle Mantel Cloth

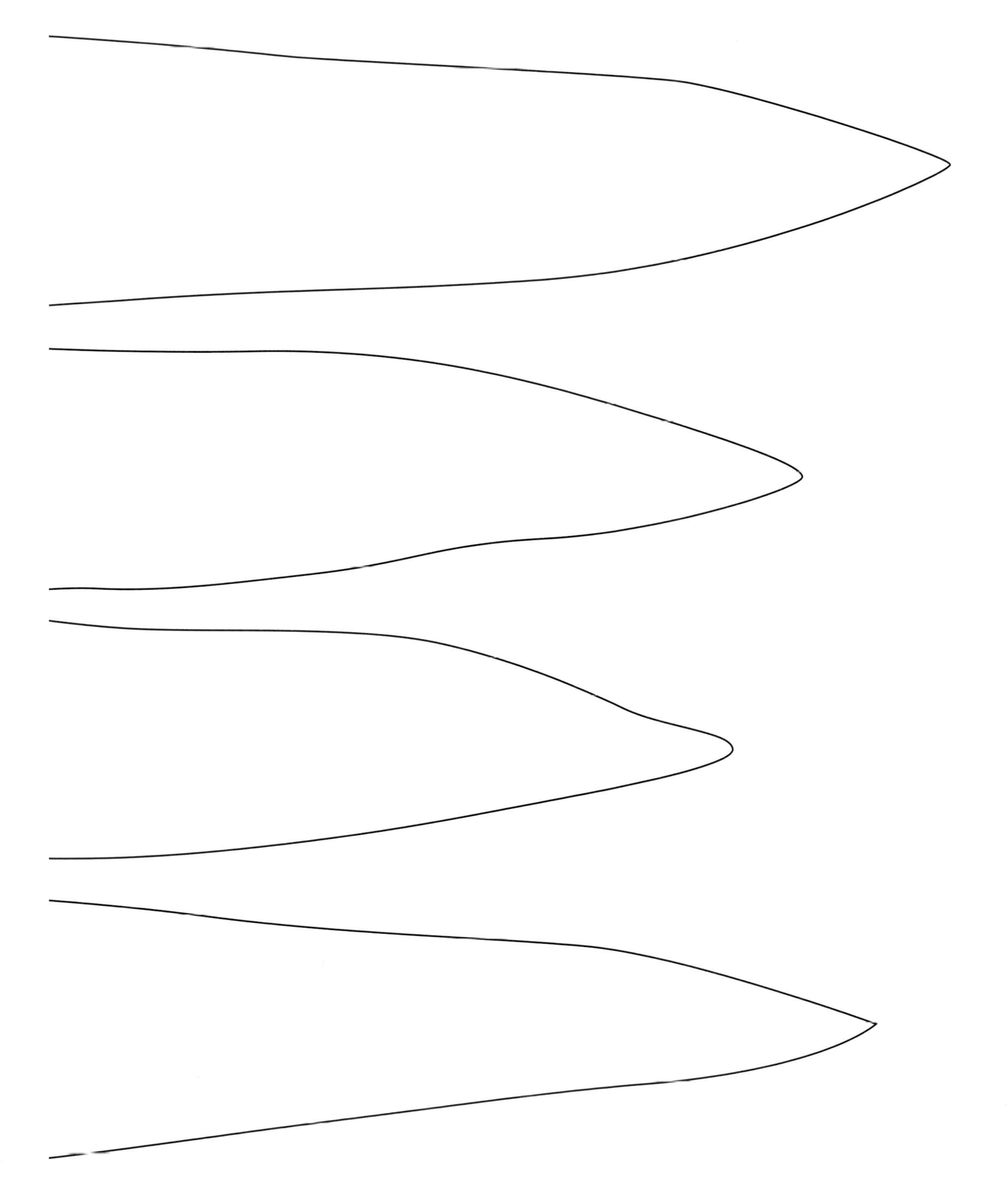

To fleece the ivory wool felt, soak the felt in warm water. Remove the excess water and machine-dry for a half hour.

Cut the Fabrics

From the muslin fabric, cut 2 body fronts and 1 body back.

From the off-white silk noil fabric, cut 2 shirtfronts, 1 shirt back, and 2 sleeves.

From the red-and-ivory plaid fabric, cut 2 skirt fronts and 1 skirt back.

From the ivory imitation fur, tear a ¾-inch-wide strip from selvage to selvage.

From the red felt, cut 2 arms, 4 shoes, and 2 hats.

From the fleeced ivory wool felt, cut 1 lower beard, 1 upper beard, 1 lower hair, 1 upper hair, 1 mustache, and 2 eyebrows.

From the red-and-white double-sided jacquard fabric, cut 1 cape.

From the red imitation fur, tear a 1-inch-wide strip from selvage to selvage.

Sew the Santa

Sew the body fronts together at the center front. Clip the curves and press the seam allowances open. Sew the body front to the body back, leaving the bottom edge open. Clip curves at the neck. Press the seam allowances open and turn the body right side out.

Firmly stuff the top three-fourths of the body with polyester fiberfill through the bottom opening. Fill the bottom one-fourth of the body with plastic pellets. If using 3-inch-diameter crescent board circles, glue the eight circles together with crafts glue. Insert the 3-inch-diameter wooden circle or the layered crescent board circle into the bottom of the body. Adjust the plastic pellets to allow for a ½-inch seam allowance at the bottom edge of the body. Hot-glue the seam allowance to the bottom of the circle.

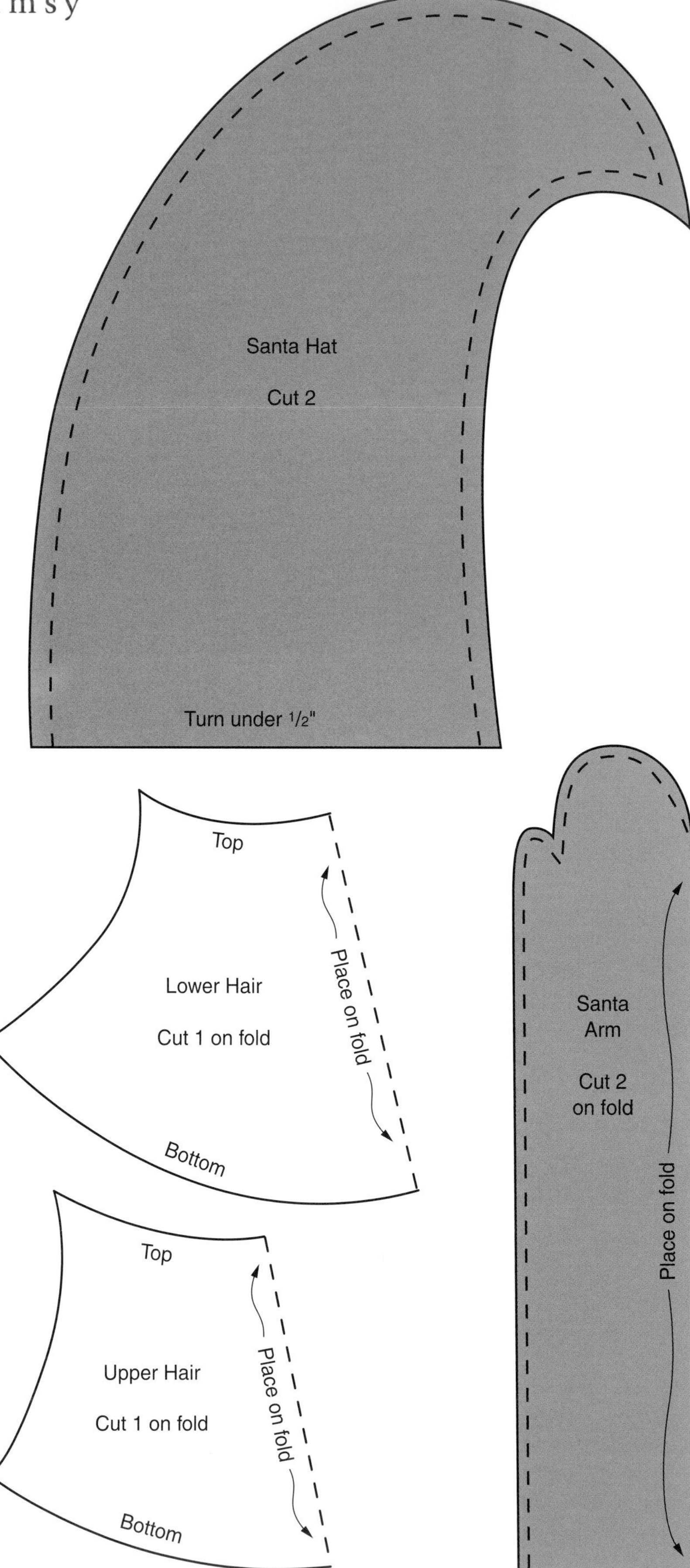

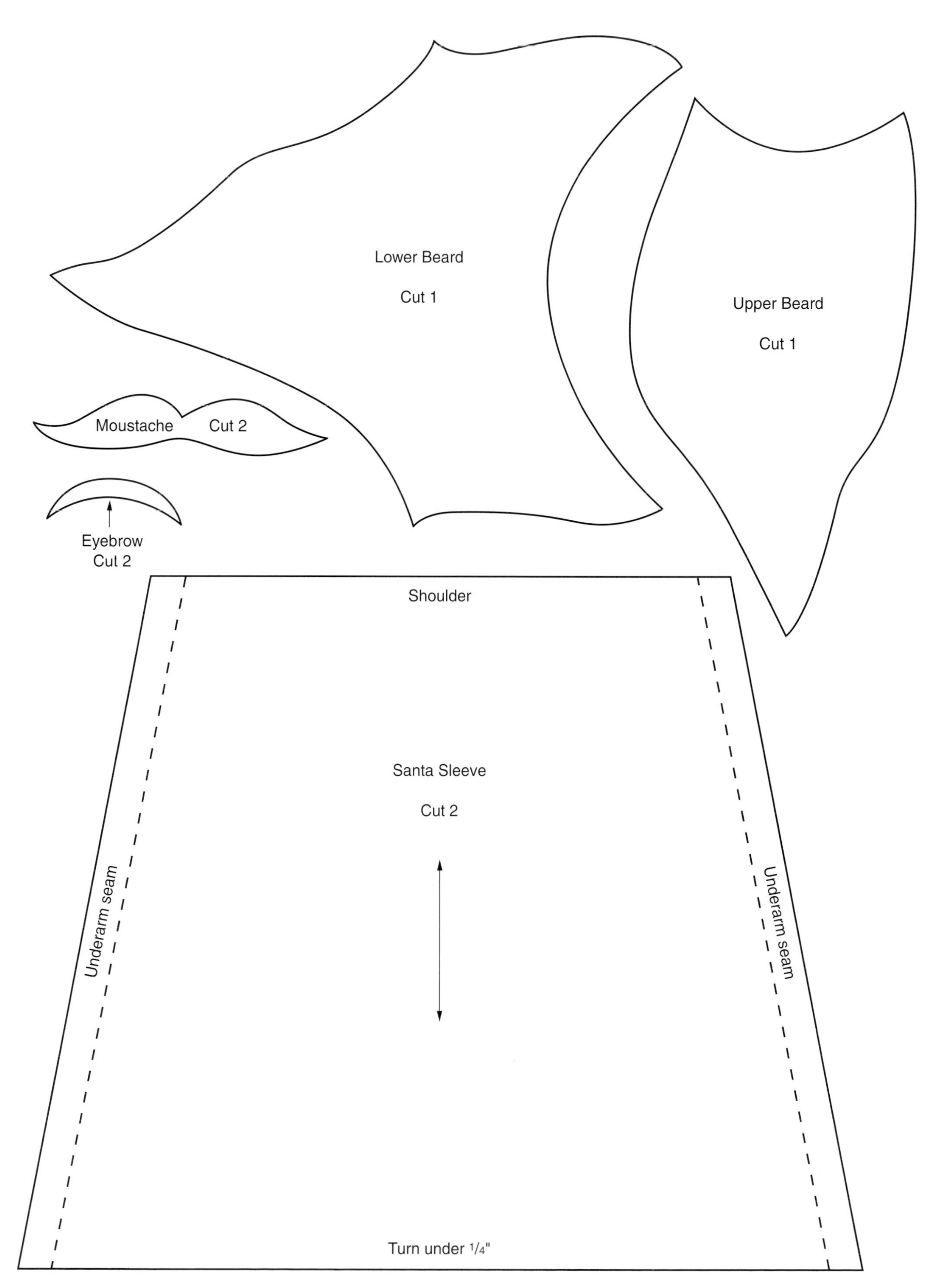
Lower Beard
Cut 1
Upper Beard
Cut 1
Moustache
Cut 2
Eyebrow
Cut 2
Shoulder
Santa Sleeve
Cut 2
Underarm seam
Underarm seam
Turn under 1/4"

Apply two coats of flesh tone paint to the head, letting the paint dry between coats. Referring to the photograph on *page 00*, use a pencil to lightly draw facial features. Paint the eyes white, add brown circles for the irises, and a tiny white highlight dot on each iris. Use red for the mouth. Mix a small amount of red with white for the cheeks. Lightly outline the eyes with the black pen.

Dress the Santa

Sew the shirtfronts together at the center front seam; press the seam allowances open. Sew the skirt fronts together at the center front seam; press the seam allowances open.

Sew the shirtfront to the skirt front at the waist, matching the center front seams. Press the seam allowances open. Sew the shirt back to the skirt back at the waist; press the seam allowance open. Sew the assembled front to the back at the side seams, leaving an opening for each sleeve as indicated on the pattern. Press the seam allowances open and turn right side out. Sew a narrow hem at the bottom edge of the skirt and slip it on the doll.

Glue ¾-inch-wide ivory fur around the bottom edge of the skirt. For the suspenders, hand-sew or glue one end of the ⅜-inch-wide red-and-white ribbon to the waist seam on one side of the shirtfront as indicated on pattern. Bring the ribbon up over one shoulder, around the back, over the second shoulder, and down to the waist seam on the opposite side of the shirtfront. Trim the excess ribbon; hand-sew or glue the end in place. Tack the suspenders to the shirt shoulders.

Use fiberfill to lightly stuff the stomach area between the shirt and the body. For the belt, glue one end of the 1-inch-wide velvet ribbon around the center post of the belt buckle. Wrap the belt snugly around the waist with the buckle at the center front. Trim the belt end at an angle and thread through the buckle, cinching in Santa's belly. Glue the belt in place on the center back. Sew the three red bells evenly spaced on the center front seam of the shirt.

With the arm folded in half lengthwise, sew $\frac{1}{16}$ inch from the cut edges, leaving the short straight edge open. Do not turn. Repeat for the second arm. Coil one end on each of two chenille stems. Insert a coiled end into each arm. Tack the chenille stems to the arm ends; do not trim the chenille stem yet. Position the arms around Santa's body. Securely twist the chenille stems together at the back so that arms are desired length and fit snugly in place; now trim any excess. Slip the arms through the sleeve openings at the side seams of the shirt.

Fold each sleeve in half and sew the underarm seam; press the seam allowances open. Turn the sleeves right sides out. To hem, turn up ¼ inch and sew close to the edge. Slip sleeves over arms and tuck into shoulder opening of shirt. Tack sleeves to shirt. Glue ¾-inch-wide ivory fur around the bottom edge of each sleeve.

Sew the shoes together in pairs with a $\frac{1}{16}$-inch seam allowance, leaving the short straight edges open. Do not turn. Cut two 4½-inch lengths of chenille stem. Coil one end of each length. Slip a chenille stem, coiled end first, into each shoe. Hot-glue about 1 inch of each shoe to the bottom of the body. To eliminate bulk, trim away one layer of felt from the glued area of each shoe. If using 3½-inch-diameter crescent board circles, glue the four circles together with crafts glue. Cover the 3½-inch-diameter wooden circle or the layered crescent board circle with a scrap of plaid fabric. Hot-glue the fabric-covered circle to the bottom of the body.

Fashion the Hair and Beard

To fringe the upper and lower hair pieces, cut slits approximately ⅛ inch apart, beginning at the bottom edge and stopping about ½ inch from the top edge. Glue the top edge of the lower hair to the back of the head so the ends rest on Santa's shoulders. Glue the upper hair to the back of the head ¾ inch above the lower hair. Glue the eyebrows in place.

Center the upper beard on the lower beard. Sew the beards together close to the edges of the upper beard, leaving the top edge open. Cut a 4-inch length of chenille stem; coil one end. Slip the coiled end between the beard layers; sew the top edge closed. Glue the beard to the face just below the mouth. Glue the mustache in place.

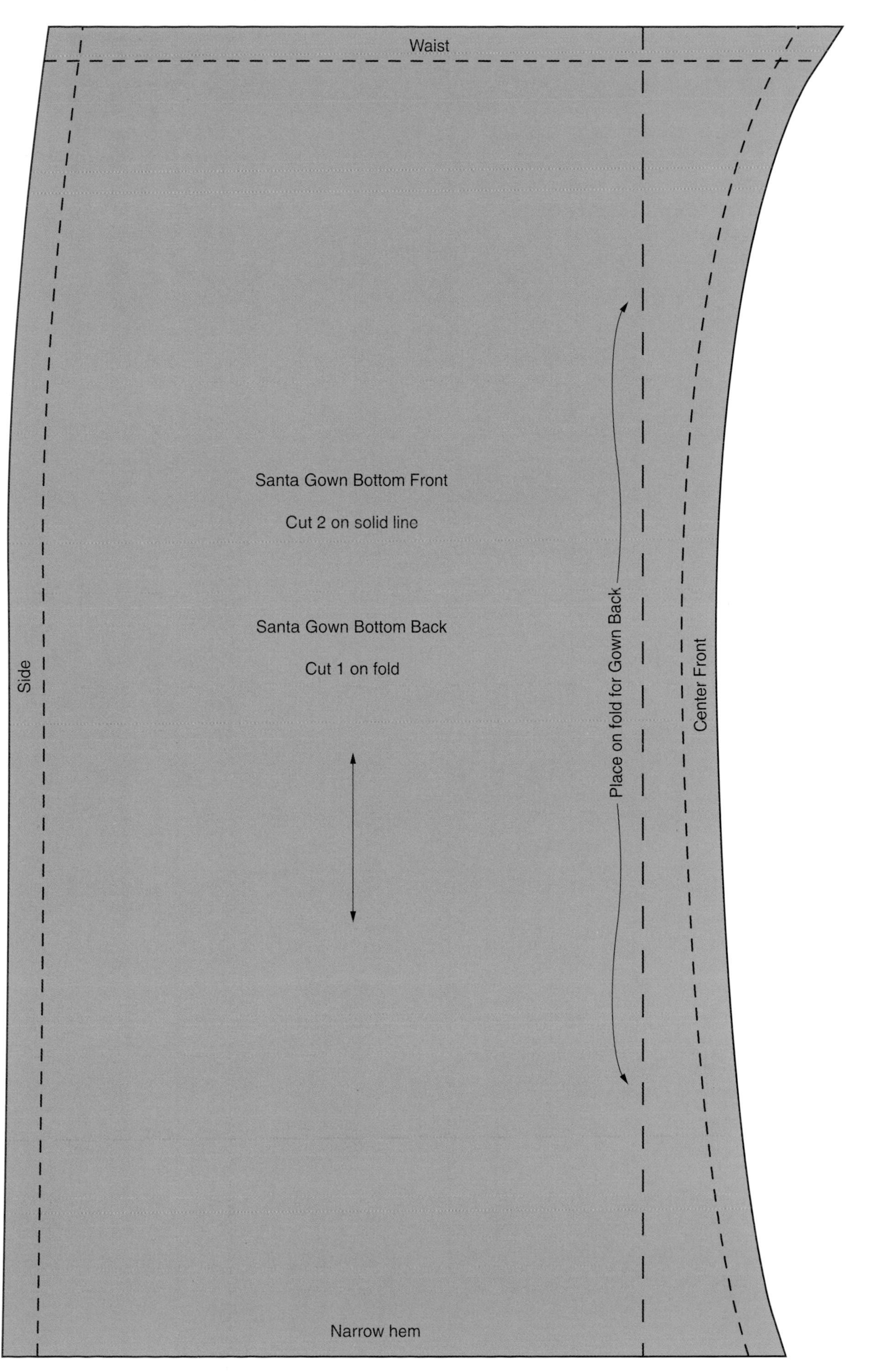
Waist
Santa Gown Bottom Front
Cut 2 on solid line
Santa Gown Bottom Back
Cut 1 on fold
Side
Place on fold for Gown Back
Center Front
Narrow hem

Add the Hat and Cape

Sew the hats together at the curved edges with a ⅛-inch seam allowance. Turn the hat right side out. Stuff the hat with fiberfill. Turn under ½ inch at the open edge of the hat and glue to the head. Glue ¾-inch-wide ivory fur over the bottom edge of the hat and around the tip.

Baste ¼ inch from the neck edge of the cape. Pull the basting threads to gather the neck area as tightly as possible; knot the thread ends. Glue 1-inch-wide red fur to the left, right, and bottom edges of the cape, folding the fur over the edges and gluing to both sides of the fabric. Use sewing thread to tie the cape around Santa's neck.

Adjust the beard, arms, and shoes as desired, shaping the hidden chenille stems. Wrap the ends of the artificial spray around the wrists.

All designs by Mary Jo Hiney

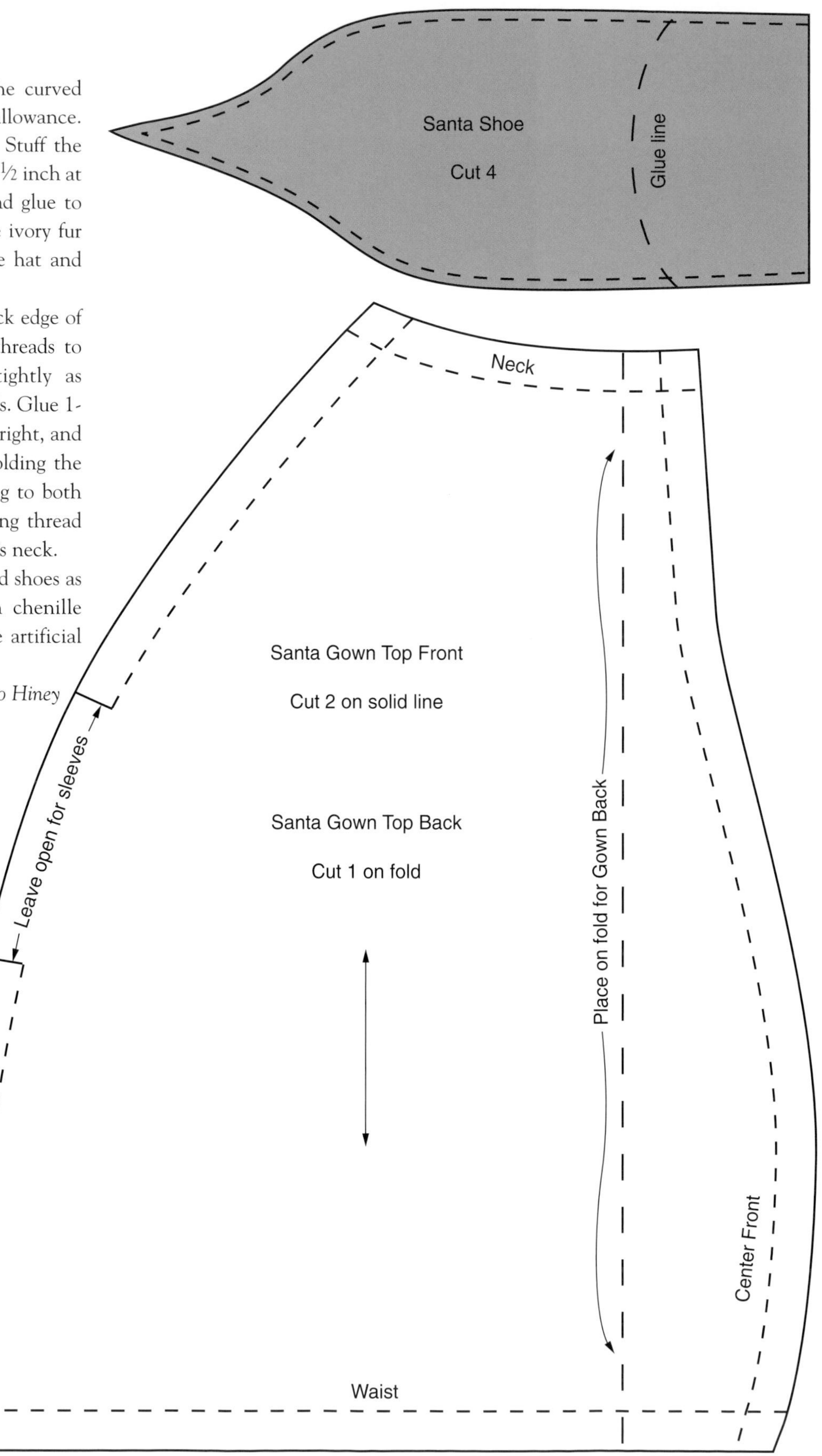

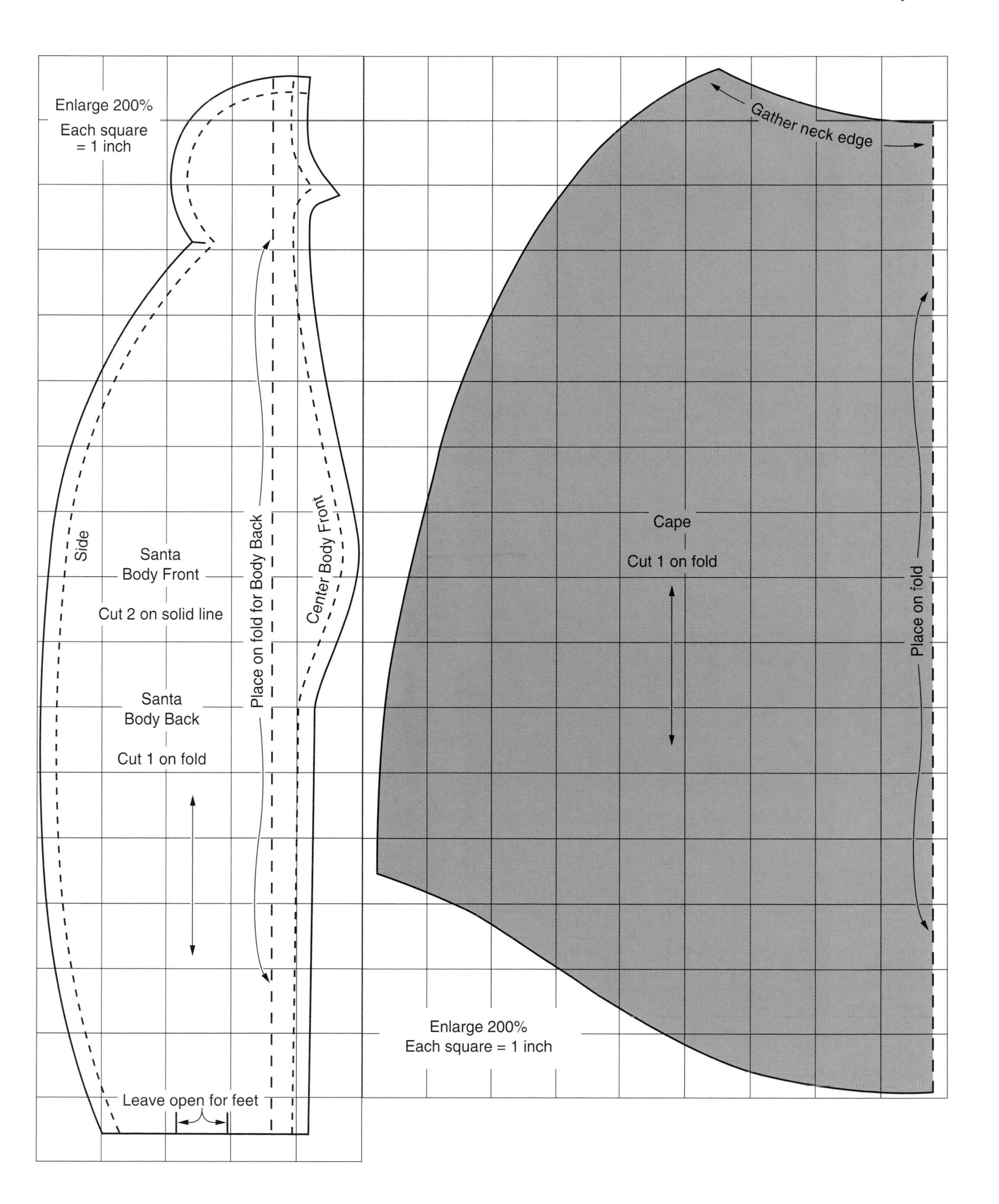
Enlarge 200%
Each square = 1 inch
Side
Santa
Body Front
Cut 2 on solid line
Santa
Body Back
Cut 1 on fold
Place on fold for Body Back
Center Body Front
Leave open for feet
Gather neck edge
Cape
Cut 1 on fold
Place on fold
Enlarge 200%
Each square = 1 inch

Cavity-Free Christmas

KIDS AND HOLIDAY TREATS go hand in hand. This year, instead of overloading in sugary snacks, why not indulge the kids' creative cravings with colorful ornaments that will satisfy even the sweetest tooth?

Children of all ages will enjoy sculpting their own versions of treats with oven-bake clay. Let smaller ones try their hand with cookie-cutter ornaments, as the bigger kids sculpt and decorate the clay to make realistic-looking sweets. A felt tree skirt with a red-and-white rickrack border fits the scene perfectly.

Reserve a special spot for a tree the kids will enjoy decorating with their own "sugar-free" creations *opposite*. These ornaments may look good enough to eat, but they'll last from year to year because they're made from clay that is baked in the oven. Not only will the kids will have a blast decorating with their ornaments this season, but in the years ahead you'll all cherish bringing out their handmade creations at Christmastime.

Could the bicycle ornament *above* be someone's hint at a Christmas wish? The bike is cut from ecru clay with a cookie cutter, then baked and decorated with dimensional paint.

Just like icing a real cookie, there's no right or wrong when it comes to making cookie-cutter ornaments such as the star *above* or the gingerbread girl *opposite, bottom left*. Simply bring out your stash of favorite holiday cutters and let your kids' imaginations run wild. They will love making each ornament unique by "icing" it with dimensional paint.

For those ready to tackle the craft of sculpting, some designs, such as the miniature ribbon candies and swirling lollipops *opposite*, require a bit more dexterity.

Reserve a special spot for a tree the kids will enjoy decorating with their own "sugar-free" creations.

Clay Ornaments

Shown on pages 68–74.

YOU WILL NEED

- Waxed paper
- Sculpey Premo polymer clay: blue pearl, burnt umber, cadmium yellow, cadmium red, cobalt blue, ecru, fuchsia, green, green pearl, orange, raw sienna, red pearl, and white
- Nonstick surface, such as a piece of poster board
- Straight-sided drinking glass or acrylic clay roller
- Cookie cutters
- Toothpicks
- Butter knife
- Miniature cupcake papers
- Aluminum foil
- Baking sheet
- Sculpey Gloss Glaze
- Sponge brush
- Assorted colors of puff paints
- Acrylic tube paints: white and dark brown
- Miniature glass marbles
- Glue gun and hotmelt adhesive
- Sucker sticks
- Beads
- Chenille stems or narrow ribbon

INSTRUCTIONS

Cover your work area with a sheet of waxed paper. Knead the clay between the palms of your hands until it is soft and pliable.

For the cutouts, place the desired color of clay on the shiny side of the nonstick surface, and use a straight-sided roller or drinking glass to roll out the clay until it is a scant 1/4 inch thick. Use the cookie cutters to cut out the desired shapes. Stick a toothpick through the center top of the cutout to make a hole for the hanger.

For ribbon-candy ornaments, roll 12-inch snakes of various diameters in the desired clay colors. Place the snakes side by side. Roll down the length of the logs with a straight-sided roller or drinking glass, joining the snakes together and increasing the length. Use a knife to cut straight edges at the top and bottom. Cut the striped clay in half. Accordion-fold each piece back and forth. Use a toothpick to make a hole through the center of the top fold of each candy.

For a sucker or candy-cane ornament, roll 1/4-inch-diameter snakes of two or three clay colors. Twist and roll the snakes together. To make a sucker, begin wrapping the twisted clay around itself, working from the center out. Make the sucker as large as you like and cut off the excess; press the wraps together. Make a hole through the center top of the sucker with a toothpick. To make a candy cane, cut a 5½-inch length of twisted snakes. Bend down one end of the clay to make a cane shape.

To make a cupcake ornament, fill the miniature cupcake papers with clay. Flatten a separate ball of clay and shape it into a mounded circle that will fit on top of the cupcake bottom. Use a toothpick to make a hole through the center top of the mound. Press the mound of clay onto the top of the clay in the cupcake paper.

For an ice-cream cone, use a straight-sided roller or drinking glass to roll out brown clay until it is a scant 1/8 inch thick. Use the dull side of a butter knife to carve a diagonal grid pattern onto the clay. Cut a small quarter-circle of the clay. Overlap the straight edges to shape the cone; press the overlapped areas together. Use a single color or mix several colors together to shape a hollow scoop for the ice cream. Use a toothpick to make a hole through the center top of the scoop. Press the scoop on the cone. Wrap a snake of clay around the bottom edge of the scoop, overlapping the cone and shaping it to look realistic.

For the candy icicles, shape brown clay into a chocolate candy shape or mix several colors together to look like a piece of hard candy. To make peppermint candies, twist together a small snake of red or green with white. Cut the twisted clay into a 1½-inch length or wrap the clay around itself to form a circle. Use a toothpick to make holes through each piece of candy.

Place the ornaments on a baking sheet covered with aluminum foil. Bake the ornaments in the oven according to the instructions on the clay package. Let the ornaments cool.

Finishing touches

For a shiny appearance on any of the ornaments, apply a coat of gloss glaze with a sponge brush following the manufacturer's instructions. Let the glaze dry.

Referring to the photographs for ideas, add details to the cutout ornaments with puff paint (sketch the details in pencil first if you like) or paint frosting on them with white acrylic tube paint. Press miniature glass marbles into the wet paint. Let the paint dry.

Hot-glue a sucker stick to the back of the sucker. Tie a chenille stem in a bow around the base of the sucker.

Frost the cupcake ornament with white acrylic tube paint. Immediately press miniature glass marbles into the wet paint. Let the paint dry.

To add a "chocolate" shell to the ice-cream cone, paint dark brown acrylic tube paint to almost cover the scoop of ice cream.

To make a candy icicle, alternate beads with two candies on a chenille stem. Bend the bottom of the stem back and forth. Make a loop with the stem at the top of the icicle; trim off the excess stem.

Insert wire ornament hangers through the holes in the ornaments or through the stem loops; bend or hot-glue the hangers in place. If you like, thread a bead onto the hanger and tie a chenille stem or ribbon bow around the hanger.

Designed by Glenda Aldrich

Felt Tree Skirt

Shown below and on page 72.

YOU WILL NEED

- 1 yard each of chartreuse and lavender felt
- 1 yard of string
- T-pin
- Fabric marking pen
- Pinking shears
- Two packages each of red and white jumbo rickrack
- Clear nylon thread

INSTRUCTIONS

Fold the chartreuse felt into quarters. Tie one end of the string to the T-pin. Tie the remaining end of the string to the marking pen, keeping 17 inches of string between the T-pin and pen. Anchor the T-pin to the center of the felt (the folded corner opposite the cut edges). Draw a partial circle on the felt with the marking pen by making an arc with the string fully extended. For the tree-trunk opening, shorten the length of string between the pen and the T-pin to 3 inches; mark the curve on the felt. Use a pinking shears to cut through all layers of the felt on the outer marked line. Cut on the inner marked line with a straight-edge scissors. For the center back opening, cut through one fold from the outer edge to the tree-trunk opening.

Fold the lavender felt into quarters. Anchor the T-pin to the center of the felt. For the tree-trunk opening, keep the string length at 3 inches and mark the curve on the fold. Lengthen the string between the pen and the T-pin to 16½ inches. Draw a partial circle on the felt. Cut through all layers of the purple felt on both marked lines with a straight-edge scissors. For the center back opening, cut through one fold to the tree-trunk opening.

Unfolding the felts, pin the lavender skirt onto the chartreuse skirt, aligning the edges of the tree-trunk openings and the center back openings.

To make the candy cane trim, twist together the red and white rickrack. Pin the trim to the tree skirt about ¼ inch from the outer edges of the lavender felt, turning under the raw ends at the center back. Thread the sewing machine with clear nylon thread. Sew the trim to the skirt down the center of the trim.

Designed by Nancy Wyatt

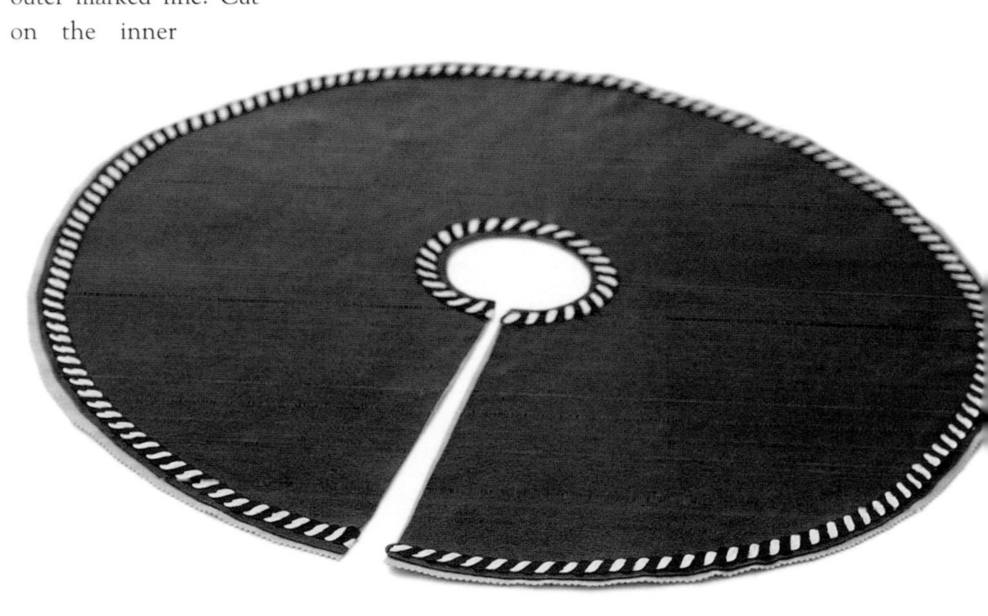

Plentiful Christmas

THE BLESSINGS OF FAMILY, food, and faith can bring life to the decorations in your home.

Immerse your tree in a profusion of nature-inspired ornaments, *opposite*. Velveteen-topped acorns, stately fleur-de-lis, and beaded cross ornaments represent important reasons for celebrating the season. Tiny bird wreaths and fabric-covered ornaments, *above*, serve as simple handcrafted tree trimmings. A fruitful display of cornucopias and wreaths, elegant stockings, and an urn bursting with nature's harvest round out the scene.

Give a lifelike artificial bird a cozy home inside a beaded berry wreath, *above*. Seed beads strung onto thin-gauge wire glitter in the light to make the wreath's "greenery," and red round beads interspersed around the ornament take on the role of berries.

Two of nature's most beautiful creations—flowers and fruit—bring sophistication to a fireplace mantel and hearth, *opposite*. Muted floral fabrics mix with unexpected check, stripe, and harlequin fabrics along the stocking cuffs, accented with beads. A grapevine wreath encircling a cast-iron urn makes a luxurious nest of artificial fruit—a delightful perch for an artificial quail.

Perfect above a mantelscape of colorful fruits and greens, the holiday wreath *left* will complement your decor throughout the winter months. Within a grapevine wreath covered with green sheet moss, fresh pomegranates nestle among sprigs of preserved and dried flowers in earthy tones of mustard, violet, and crimson.

Miniature cornucopias take shape with the help of chicken wire filled with Spanish moss, *above*. Inside the cone, a plastic-foam ball secures the bounty of artificial grapes, berries, and leaves.

Cornucopia Ornament

Shown at right and on page 81.

YOU WILL NEED

- 10-inch square of ½-inch mesh chicken wire
- Wire cutters
- Spray paints: rust and brown
- 2- and 3-inch-diameter Styrofoam plastic-foam balls
- Green planter's moss
- Tacky glue
- Glue gun and hotmelt adhesive
- Wooden skewer
- Gardening gloves
- 24-gauge green florist's wire
- Five large bay leaves
- Three bunches of small artificial grapes
- E6000 adhesive
- Three sprigs of artificial boysenberries
- Reindeer moss
- Spanish moss

INSTRUCTIONS

Note: *To protect your hands from cuts while working with the chicken wire, wear a pair of gardening gloves.* Round one corner of the chicken wire square with the wire cutters for the bottom open edge of the cornucopia. Spray the chicken wire with both the brown and rust paints, letting the paint dry between coats.

Cut the 3-inch-diameter plastic-foam ball in half; set aside one half for another project. Glue green planter's moss over all surfaces of the 2-inch plastic-foam ball and the half-ball with tacky glue. When the glue is dry, hot-glue the flat side of the half-ball to the 2-inch ball. Push the wooden skewer through the center of the plastic-foam pieces to secure. Trim the skewer even with the pieces and set aside.

Place the painted chicken wire wrong side up on your work surface. Place a layer of green planter's moss over the chicken wire. Wearing gloves, bend the chicken wire into a cone shape, creating a 5-inch-diameter opening with the rounded corner at the bottom of the opening. Use florist's wire to secure the overlapping edges of the chicken wire. Trim away the excess wire and bend the cut ends into the cone. Shape the cone into a cornucopia shape.

Insert and hot-glue the 2-inch ball end of the plastic-foam pieces into the cornucopia. Hot-glue the bay leaves to overlap inside the cornucopia along the bottom edge of the opening. Cut several 10-inch lengths of florist's wire. Fold and twist the wire lengths around the grape bunches. Insert and glue the wire ends into the plastic-foam with the adhesive. Glue boysenberry sprigs in the plastic foam among the grapes with the adhesive. Hot-glue small amounts of reindeer and Spanish moss to the cornucopia opening.

Large Acorn Ornament

Shown at left and on page 76.

YOU WILL NEED

- Tracing paper
- ¼ yard of bold Jacobean-designed jacquard fabric
- 5-inch-long Styrofoam plastic-foam egg
- Tape measure and pencil
- Foam glue
- Straight pins
- ½ yard of ½-inch-wide burgundy velvet ribbon
- 7-inch-diameter circle of mustard gold velveteen

- Gold sewing thread; needle
- Polyester fiberfill
- Green planter's moss
- Beads: 25 size 11/0 silver-lined purple seed, ten red bugle, and 30 silver-lined terra-cotta seed
- 12-inch length of 24-gauge silver wire
- Wooden skewer
- Wire cutters
- E6000 adhesive

INSTRUCTIONS

Trace the acorn pattern *below*. Cut out the pattern. Use the pattern to cut two shapes from the jacquard fabric.

Use a pencil and the tape measure to make marks horizontally around the egg 3 inches from the center of the wide end. Position the wrong side of a fabric shape on one half of the egg with the tip of the fabric at the center of the narrow end and the straight fabric edge just above the pencil marks. Glue and pin the fabric to the egg with foam glue, stretching the fabric snug against the egg. Repeat with the second fabric shape on the opposite half of the egg; if necessary trim the fabric so it won't overlap. Glue the velvet ribbon over the raw curved edges of the fabric, completely covering them.

For the acorn top, fold the velveteen circle into quarters and mark the fabric edges at the folds. Thread a needle with a long length of thread; knot the ends together to double the thread. Make running stitches ⅛ inch from the edges of the velveteen circle. Place the fabric circle over the wide end of the egg. Pull on the thread so that the fabric curves, gathering the bottom edge to fit around the egg. Adjust the fabric on the egg so that the fold marks are aligned with the velvet ribbon and centered between the ribbon ends. Pin and glue the gathered edge of the fabric circle to the egg, slightly overlapping the jacquard fabric shapes and leaving an opening for stuffing.

Stuff the top of the acorn along the outer edges with polyester fiberfill. Glue and pin the opening closed. Glue planter's moss around the egg, covering the fabric edges. Slip silver-lined purple seed beads onto straight pins; push the pins into the top of the acorn.

For the hanging loop, thread the bugle and terra-cotta seed beads onto the silver wire, alternating a bugle bead with three terra-cotta seed beads. Bend the beaded wire to form a loop. Twist the wire ends together below the beads and trim the twisted area to 1 inch. Use the skewer to puncture a hole in the center top of the acorn. Insert and glue the wire ends into the hole with the adhesive.

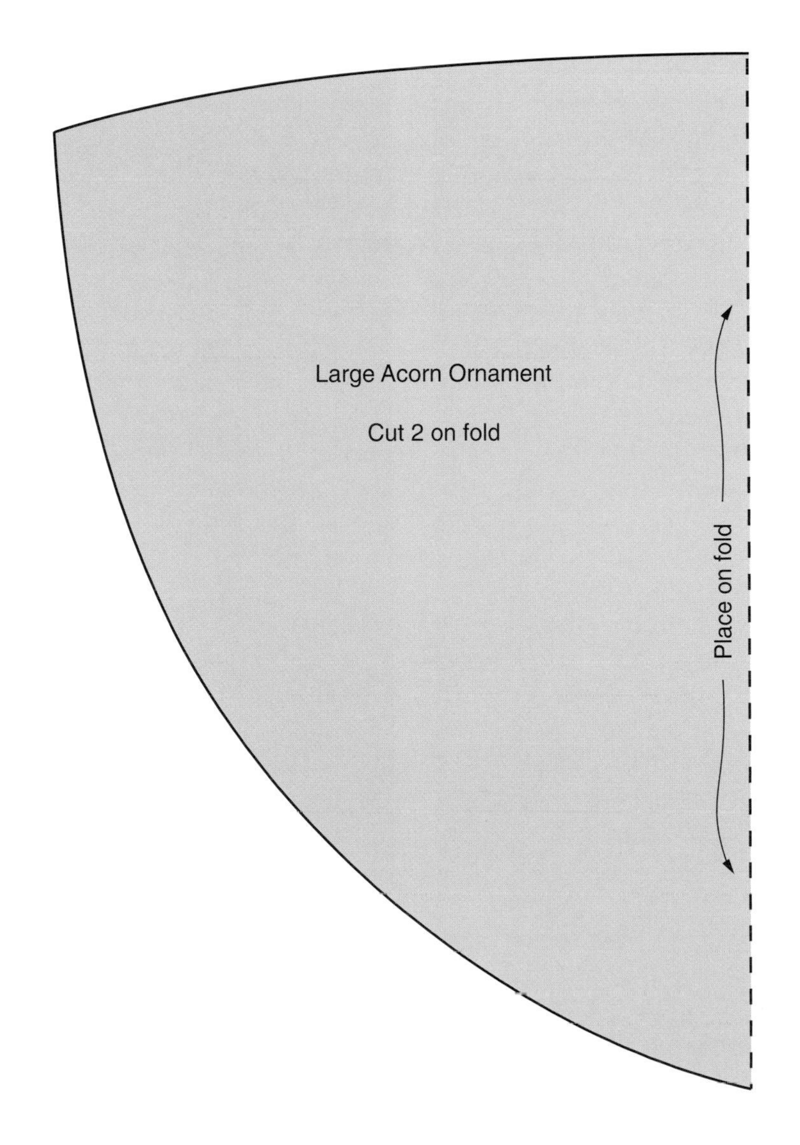

Bird Wreath Ornament

Shown on pages 78 and 84.

YOU WILL NEED

- 3¾ yards of 24-gauge silver wire
- Wire cutters
- Beads: red bugle, size 11/0 silver-lined lime rainbow matte seed, size 11/0 silver-lined green rainbow seed, ten light rust 5-millimeter round, ten rust

5-millimeter round, and three 8-millimeter red round
- Medium-size artificial bird
- Spray adhesive
- Silver glitter
- Large-eye darning needle
- ¼ yard of 4-millimeter-wide hunter green silk ribbon
- ½ yard of 4-millimeter-wide red silk ribbon
- Tacky glue

INSTRUCTIONS

Cut the silver wire into two 54-inch lengths and one 27-inch length. Working with one 54-inch length, thread in order one bugle, ten lime seeds, one rust round, ten green seeds, and another bugle onto one end of the wire. Center the beads on the wire and bend the beaded area to align the bugle beads, creating a small loop. Twist the wires together next to the bugle beads, securing the loop. Twist the loop, creating the first twisted loop.

Thread the same sequence of beads onto one end of the wire, substituting a light rust round bead for the rust bead. Slide the beads on the wire until they are next to the first loop. Bend the beaded area to create a second loop. Twist the wire twice around itself at the bottom of the new beaded loop. Twist the loop, completing the second twisted loop.

To make a twisted bead space, thread ten lime seed beads onto one end of the wire and ten green seed beads onto the other end. Slide the beads down the wires so they are next to the base of the second twisted loop. Twist the two wires together next to the seed beads, allowing the lime and green beaded areas also to twist around each other to create a twisted bead space after the loop.

Working with the longer wire, make another twisted loop in the same manner as the first. Make a twisted bead space, using both wires. Continue making twisted loops on the longer wire and twisted bead spaces on both wires to complete ten loops and nine spaces, alternating the colors of the 5-millimeter round beads.

For the top of the wreath, insert both wire ends through one 8-millimeter red bead, and then make a twisted bead space. Repeat two more times. To add the second wire length, thread and center the previously set-aside wire through the last twisted bead space. Fold the new wire in half and twist the halves together next to the beads, securing the new length. Wrap the ends of the first wire several times around the last twisted bead space; trim the excess.

Repeat the steps to make an additional ten twisted loops alternating with nine twisted bead spaces. To complete the beaded wreath, thread three bugles and ten green seed beads on one wire end, alternating one bugle and five seed beads. Thread fifteen lime seed beads and two bugles onto the second wire, alternating five seed beads and one bugle. Twist the wires together next to the beads. Twist the wire ends around the first twisted loop on the first wire to make a beaded circle. Trim the excess wire.

Lightly spray the bird with adhesive. Immediately sprinkle a small amount of glitter onto the bird. Use the darning needle to make a hole through the bird from behind the head to the center bottom.

Bend the center of the remaining wire over the top of the wreath next to the center 8-millimeter red round bead. Twist the wire halves together.

Thread eight seed beads onto one end of the wire. Twist that wire around the wreath on the other side of the center 8-millimeter bead. Randomly thread bugle and seed beads onto each wire until the beaded areas measure 1½ inches. Twist the wires together below the last beads. Twist the newly beaded areas together. Push the wires through the hole in the bird until the bird is against the beaded area. Twist

the wires together below the bird. Thread on a few beads. Twist the ends together; trim the excess wire.

For the hanging loop, tie the ends of the 4-millimeter-wide hunter green ribbon around the top of the wreath next to the first and third 8-millimeter round beads. Tie a bow with the 4-millimeter-wide red ribbon; glue the bow over the hole on the bird's back.

Fabric-Covered Ball Ornament

Shown opposite and on page 77.

YOU WILL NEED

- Tracing paper
- 1/4 yard of terra-cotta jacquard print fabric
- 5-inch Styrofoam plastic-foam ball
- Straight pins
- 1 1/8 yards of 5/8-inch-wide olive-green trim
- Vintage cherry cluster with fabric stems
- Green planter's moss
- Two small red rosebuds
- Glue gun and hotmelt adhesive

INSTRUCTIONS

Trace the wedge pattern *right* onto tracing paper. Cut out the pattern piece. Use the pattern to cut four shapes from the jacquard print fabric.

Position the fabric shapes wrong side down on the ball. Pin the shapes to the ball along all the edges with straight pins, spacing the pins about 1/4 inch apart. Pin one end of the trim to the center top of the ball where all the fabric shapes meet. Snugly wrap the trim once around the ball, covering the fabric edges; pin in place at the center top. Miter the trim and snugly wrap it around the ball again, covering the remaining fabric edges. Pin the trim in place at the center top; do not cut the excess.

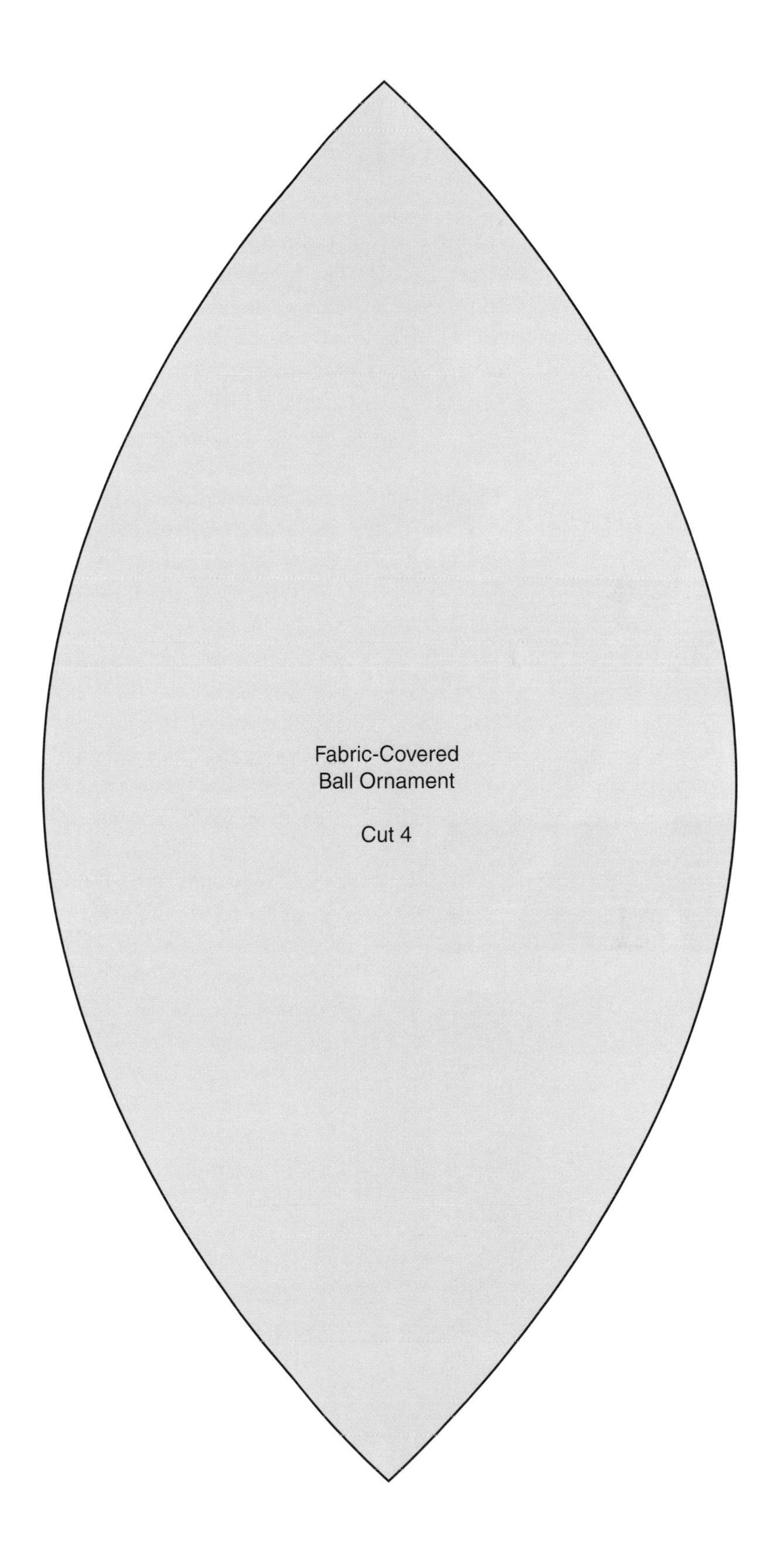

Pin the center of the cherry cluster to the center top of the ornament, letting the cherries fall over the ball top. For a hanging loop, fold the remaining trim in half, creating a loop; pin the trim end to the center top. Hot-glue a small amount of green planter's moss and two small rosebuds to the top of the ornament, covering the trim ends.

Cross Ornament

Shown below and on page 76.

YOU WILL NEED

- Sheet of black embossed paper
- Spray paint: gray metallic hammered-finish
- Paper toweling
- Tracing paper
- 7×9-inch piece of crescent board
- Crafts knife
- Crafts scissors
- Tacky glue
- 1-inch-wide sponge brush
- 9-inch length of black narrow trim
- 3/8 yard of 1/2-inch-wide antique-silver metallic trim
- Flat round silver beads: three 1/2-inch-diameter and eight 1/4-inch-diameter
- E6000 adhesive

INSTRUCTIONS

Lightly spray the black embossed paper with two coats of gray metallic hammered-finish paint, letting the paint dry between coats. Immediately wipe with paper towels, creating an uneven finish. Let dry.

Trace the cross pattern *opposite* onto tracing paper; cut out the pattern. Trace the pattern once onto the crescent board and twice onto the embossed paper. Cut out the crescent-board shape with the crafts knife and the paper shapes with a crafts scissors.

Center and glue the wrong side of one paper cross to the crescent-board cross with tacky glue and a sponge brush. For the hanging loop, glue the ends of the narrow trim on the crescent-board side of the layered cross at the upper inside corners of the center section. Center and glue the wrong side of the second paper cross to the other side of the crescent-board cross, covering the trim ends. Tie a knot in the hanging loop on the ornament back about 2 inches from the center of the trim.

Cut the antique-silver metallic trim in half. Wrap each trim length diagonally around the center section of the cross, trimming the ends to meet at the center front; glue in place. Glue a 1/2-inch-diameter silver bead at the center front of the wrapped trim with E6000 adhesive, covering the trim ends. Glue the remaining 1/2-inch-diameter beads at the top and bottom centers of the ornament front. Glue the 1/4-inch-diameter beads on the ornament front, positioning them in twos 1/4 inch apart between the two pieces of silver trim.

Fruit Topiary

Shown above and on page 76.

YOU WILL NEED

- 2 1/2×3-inch silver bucket
- Gray metallic hammered-finish spray paint
- Rock to fit inside bucket
- E6000 adhesive
- Green plastic foam
- Foam glue
- Frosted artificial pear or apple
- 8-inch length of a 1/8-inch-diameter twig
- Green planter's moss
- Reindeer moss

INSTRUCTIONS

Spray the bucket with two coats of gray metallic hammered-finish paint, letting the paint dry between coats. Glue the rock to the inside bottom of the bucket with E6000 adhesive. Cut the plastic foam to mound just above

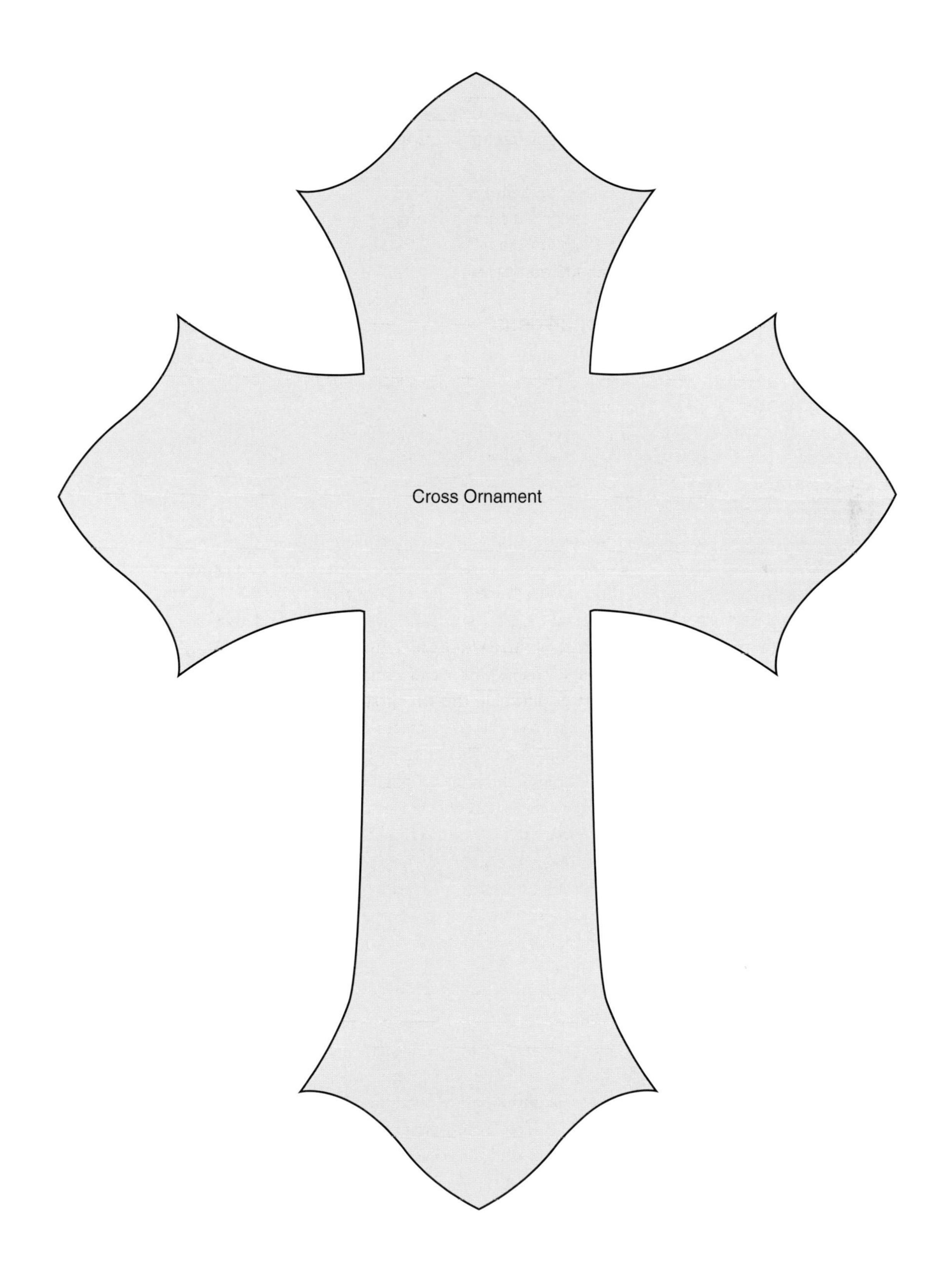
Cross Ornament

the top rim of the bucket; glue it in the bucket with the foam glue.

Insert and glue one end of the twig into the bottom of the pear or apple. Insert and glue the opposite twig end into the center of the plastic foam. Glue moss to completely cover the plastic foam.

Decoupage Ball Ornament

Shown right and on page 76.

YOU WILL NEED

- 1/4 yard of brown/ecru print cotton toile fabric
- Mod Podge decoupage medium
- Sponge brush
- 5-inch Styrofoam plastic-foam ball
- Straight pins
- 2×16-inch length of brown print cotton fabric or cotton ribbon
- 9-inch length of brown narrow trim
- Three acorn pips
- Foam glue
- Small sprig of eucalyptus and eucalyptus leaves
- Two star anise
- Glue gun and hotmelt adhesive

INSTRUCTIONS

Cut two 7 1/4-inch-diameter circles of the toile fabric, centering a design in each circle. Use the sponge brush to apply a light coat of decoupage medium to the wrong side of one fabric circle. Position the coated side of the circle onto one half of the plastic-foam ball. Pin the fabric to the ball at the center top and bottom with straight pins, stretching the fabric snug against the ball. Pin the fabric to the ball at the center of the right and left edges. Pin the fabric to the ball at spots centered between the previous pins. Continue to stretch and pin the fabric to the ball, working diagonally from side to side and making tiny pleats in the fabric so the fabric lays flat on the ball. Repeat for the second fabric circle on the opposite half of the ball.

Press under 1/2 inch on each long edge of the 2×16-inch fabric strip or ribbon. Pin one end of the strip to the center top of the ball. Snugly wrap the fabric strip or ribbon around the ball, covering the pinned fabric edges. Pin the opposite end of the fabric strip or ribbon to the center top of the ball.

For the hanging loop, fold the 9-inch length of brown narrow trim in half, forming a loop. Pin the loop ends to the center top of the ball.

Twist the acorn-pip wires together. Make a small hole in the fabric at the center top of the ornament. Insert and glue the wire ends of the pips into the hole with foam glue. Insert and glue the eucalyptus sprig into the top of the ornament. Hot-glue the eucalyptus leaves around the pips; then hot-glue the star anise on the leaves.

Fleur-de-Lis Ornament

Shown below left and on page 77.

YOU WILL NEED

- Sheet of ivory embossed paper
- Spray paint: gray metallic hammered-finish
- Acrylic paints: light terra-cotta and rust metallic
- Paintbrush; paper toweling
- Tracing paper
- 6×8-inch piece of poster board
- Crafts scissors
- Tacky glue
- 1-inch-wide sponge brush
- 9-inch length of brown narrow trim
- 1/8-inch hole punch
- Five 3/16-inch pewter eyelets
- Grommet tool and hammer
- Dark purple fine-tip permanent marker
- 12-inch length of 26-gauge brown metallic wire
- Needle-nose pliers
- Three amber or green grape cluster glass beads
- Wire cutters

INSTRUCTIONS

Lightly spray the ivory embossed paper randomly with gray metallic hammered-finish paint; let the paint dry. Brush light terra-cotta paint lightly onto the paper. Immediately wipe with a paper towel, leaving some ivory areas unpainted. Repeat with the rust metallic paint. Let the paint dry.

Trace the fleur-de-lis pattern *below* onto tracing paper. Cut out the pattern shape. Trace the pattern once onto poster board and twice onto the painted embossed paper. Cut out the shapes with a crafts scissors.

Center and glue the wrong side of one paper shape to the poster-board shape with tacky glue and a sponge brush. For the hanging loop, glue the ends of the narrow trim on the poster-board side of the layered shapes at the upper inside corners of the center section. Center and glue the wrong side of the second paper shape to the remaining side of the poster-board shape, covering the trim ends. Tie a knot in the hanging loop on the ornament back about 2 inches from the center of the trim.

Make five holes in the ornament with the 1/8-inch hole punch as indicated on the pattern. Push an eyelet through each hole. Use the grommet tool and hammer to attach each one in place from the wrong side.

Use the dark purple marker to write "be fruitful...in love...in joy...in peace...in patience...in kindness...in goodness..." along the upper edges of the ornament front.

Attach a grape cluster bead at the center bottom and the two upper eyelets. To attach a bead, wrap one end of the wire several times around the tip of the needle-nose pliers to coil. Slip the opposite end of the wire through a bead and then through an eyelet. Pull the wire until the bead dangles slightly below the ornament. Bend the wire down toward the bead and wrap it around itself in the space between the layered shape and the bead. Trim the excess wire.

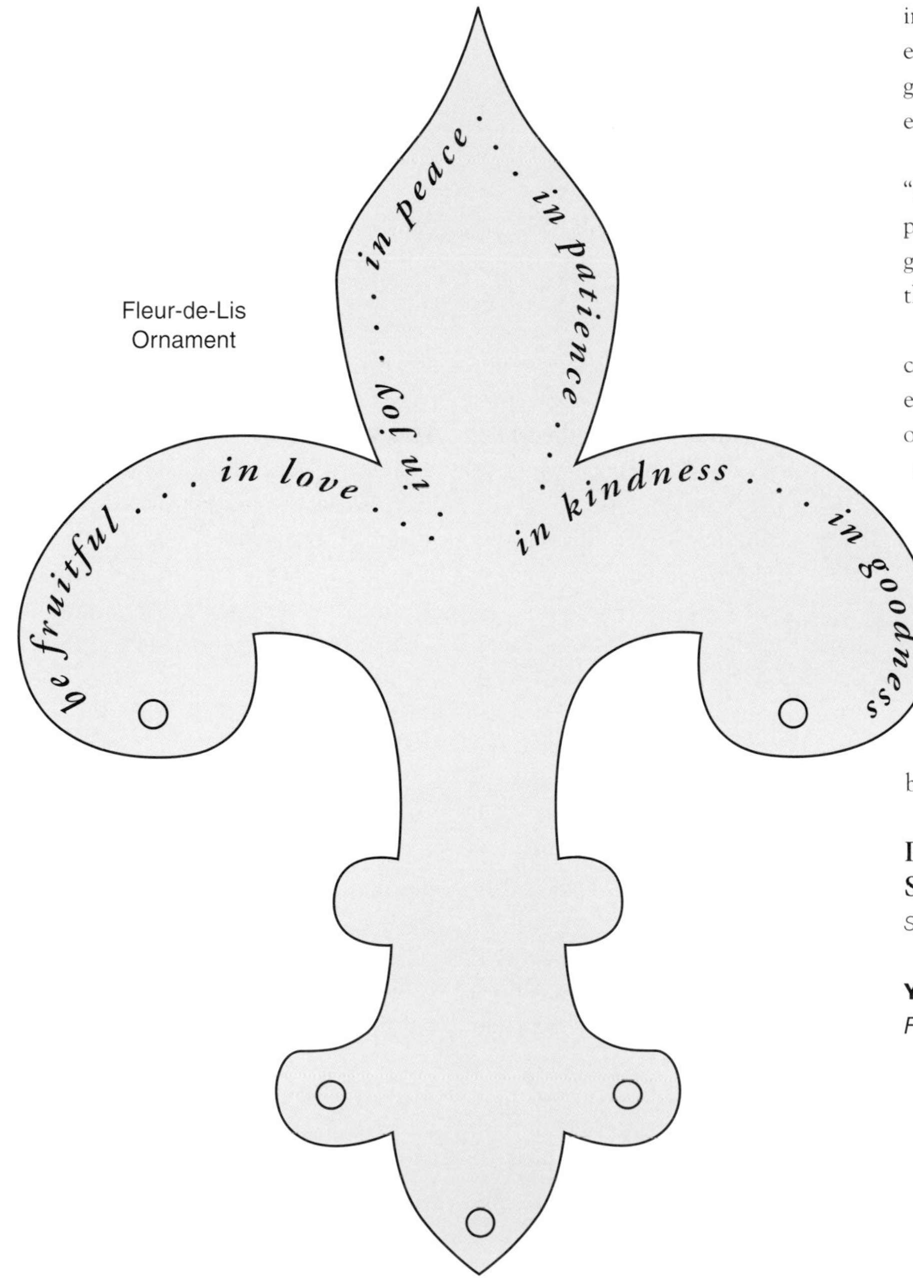

Fleur-de-Lis Ornament

Pieced-Cuff Christmas Stockings

Shown on pages 79 and 93.

YOU WILL NEED

For each stocking:

- Graph paper
- Matching sewing threads
- Pear or grape glass beads
- Red and green seed beads
- Beading needle

For the terra-cotta stocking:
- 5/8 yard of terra-cotta print jacquard fabric
- 1/8 yard each of black linen and curry gold embroidered fabrics
- 1/4 yard of pale gold linen fabric

For the gold stocking:
- 5/8 yard of ecru print jacquard fabric
- 1/4 yard each of curry-gold-embroidered and pale gold linen fabrics
- 2-inch-diameter circle template
- Erasable fabric marker

For the green stocking:
- 5/8 yard of green print jacquard fabric
- 1/8 yard each of black linen and curry-gold-embroidered fabrics
- 1/4 yard of pale gold linen fabric

For the red stocking:
- 5/8 yard of red print jacquard fabric
- 1/4 yard of curry-gold-embroidered fabric

INSTRUCTIONS

Enlarge the stocking pattern onto graph paper. Cut out the pattern piece. Sew all pieces with right sides together, using 1/4-inch seam allowances unless otherwise noted.

Cut the Fabric

Terra-Cotta Stocking: From the print jacquard, cut two stockings. From black linen, cut six 3½-inch squares. From the curry-gold-embroidered fabric, cut six 3½-inch squares and one

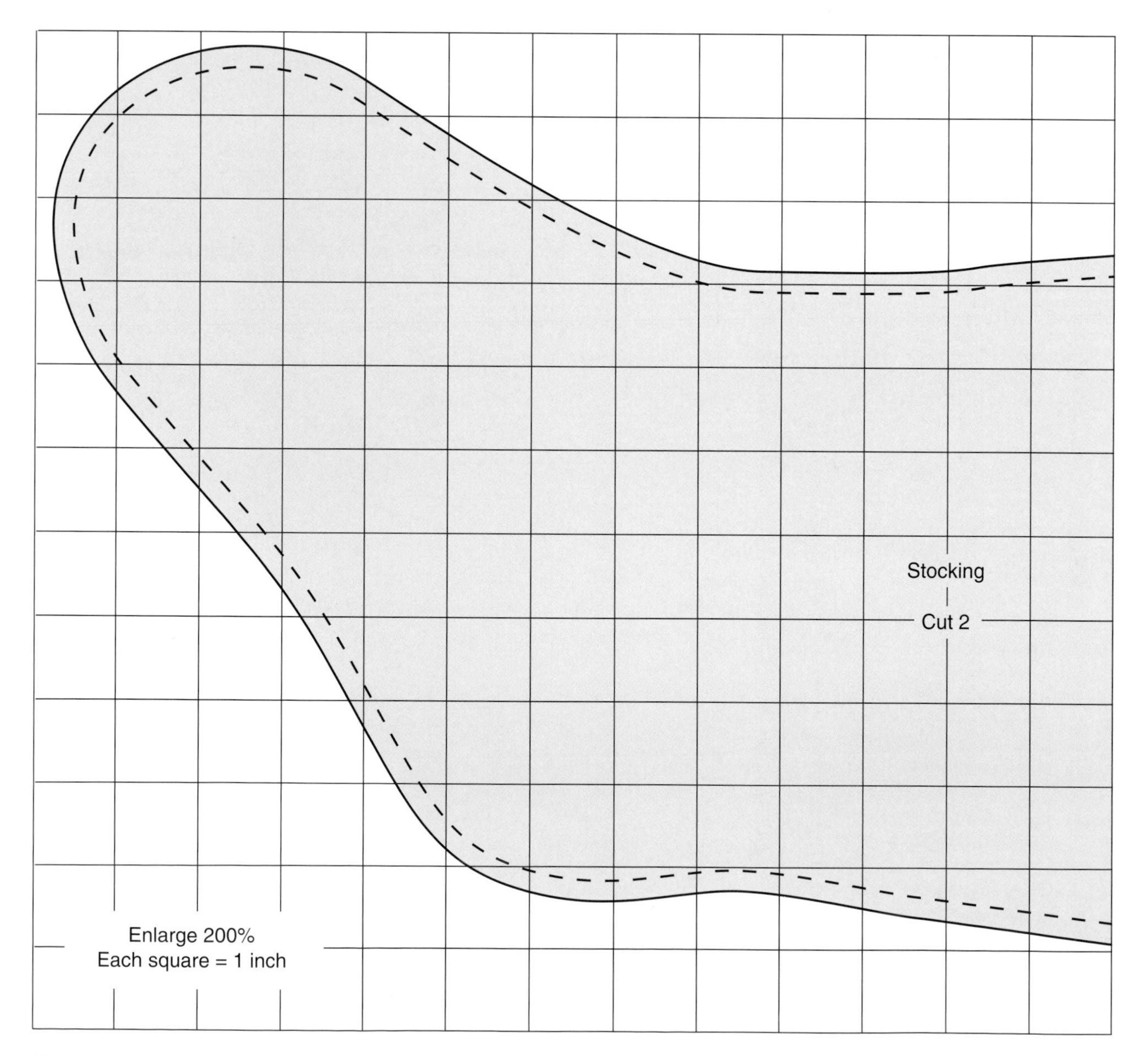

2×6-inch hanging loop strip. From the pale gold linen, cut one 7×19-inch cuff lining/border.

Ecru Stocking: From the print jacquard, cut two stockings. From the curry-gold-embroidered fabric, cut five 2⁵⁄16×6-inch strips and one 2×6-inch hanging loop. From the pale gold linen, cut one 6×19-inch cuff lining and five 2⁵⁄16×6-inch strips.

Green Stocking: From the print jacquard, cut two stockings. From the pale gold linen, cut one 7½×19-inch cuff lining/border and six 2⁵⁄16-inch squares. From the black linen, cut six 2⁵⁄16-inch squares and one 2×6-inch hanging loop strip. From the curry-gold-embroidered fabric, cut six 2⁵⁄16-inch squares.

Red Stocking: From the print jacquard, cut two stockings, one 4½×19-inch cuff, and one 2×6-inch hanging loop strip. **Note:** *Use the reverse side of the jacquard for the cuff front and hanging loop*. From the curry-gold-embroidered fabric, cut one 7½×19-inch cuff lining/border.

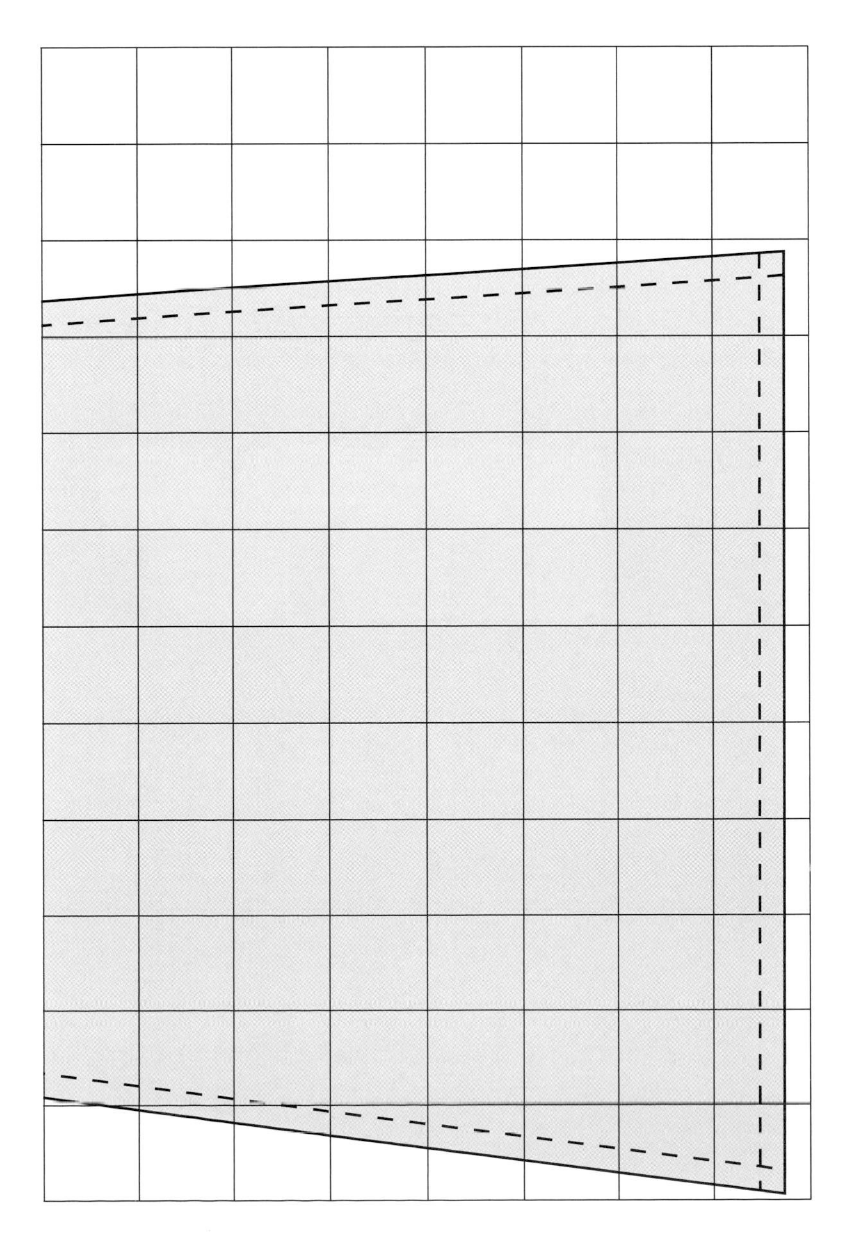

Sew the Stocking

Sew the stocking front to the back, leaving the top edge open. Zigzag-stitch or overcast the seam allowances together. Clip the curves. Press the seam allowances toward the back as much as possible. Turn the stocking right side out.

For the hanging loop, press under ½ inch on the long edges of the 2×6-inch strip. **Note:** *For the red stocking, we used the reverse side of the jacquard strip as the right side of the fabric*. Fold the strip in half lengthwise, aligning the pressed edges; press again. Sew the long edges together opposite the fold. Fold the strip in half, forming the loop. Baste the ends to the top inside corner on the heel side of the stocking with the loop inside the stocking.

Refer to "Sew the Cuffs" on *page 92* for instructions to assemble the desired cuff for the stocking.

Slip the cuff inside the stocking with the right side of the cuff facing the wrong side of the stocking, aligning the raw edges. Sew the top edges together with a ½-inch seam allowance. Trim the seam allowance to ¼ inch. Zigzag-stitch or overcast the seam allowances. Press the seam allowance toward the cuff. Fold the cuff to the outside of the stocking.

Referring to the photographs on *page 79* and *page 93* for placement ideas, sew bead fringe to the corners, points, scallops, or centers of the cuffs. For each bead fringe, knot thread in a beading needle, and come out at the desired point on the cuff. Thread the desired number and color of seed beads on the needle, then a pear or grape bead, and finish with the reversed pattern of seed beads. Return the needle back to the same location on the cuff, and knot on the wrong side. For the red stocking, gather up the border fabric at the center front of the cuff when attaching the bead fringe.

Sew the Cuff

Terra-Cotta Stocking: Sew the 3½-inch squares together in two rows of six squares, pressing the seam allowances open and alternating the black and curry gold squares in a checkerboard fashion. Sew together the short edges of the pieced cuff, forming a circle. Press the seam allowances open. Sew together the short edges of the pale gold cuff lining/border. Press the seam allowances open and turn right side out. Slip the cuff lining into the pieced cuff with right sides together. Align and sew the bottom edges together. Press the seam allowances toward the lining. Turn the cuff right side out; press, aligning the top edges to create a ¼-inch pale gold border at the bottom. Baste the top edges together.

Gold Stocking: Sew the long edges of the curry gold and pale gold strips together, alternating the colors and forming a circle. To make scallops, use the erasable fabric marker to trace around the circle template at the bottom edge on the wrong side of each fabric strip. Sew together the short edges of the pale gold cuff lining. Press the seam allowances open and turn right side out.

Slip the lining into the pieced cuff with right sides together. Align and sew the bottom edges together on the traced scallop lines, using a very short stitch length. Trim the seam allowances and clip curves. Turn the cuff right side out and press. Baste the top edges together.

Green Stocking: Sew a pale gold square and a black square to opposite edges of each gold-embroidered square to make six rows of three squares. Press the seam allowances toward the gold embroidered squares. Offset the rows by one square to sew a pale gold square to a gold-embroidered square and a gold-embroidered square to a black square. Sew the first and the last rows together, forming a circle. Trim away the excess triangle portion at the top and bottom edges of the pieced cuff, leaving a ¼-inch seam allowance along each edge.

Sew together the short edges of the pale cuff lining/border. Press the seam allowances open and turn right side out. Slip the lining into the pieced cuff with right sides together. Align and sew the bottom edges together. Press the seam allowances toward the lining. Turn the cuff right side out; press, aligning the top edges to create a 1-inch pale gold border at the bottom. Baste the top edges together.

Red Stocking: Using the wrong side of the jacquard fabric as the right side of the cuff, sew one long edge of the cuff

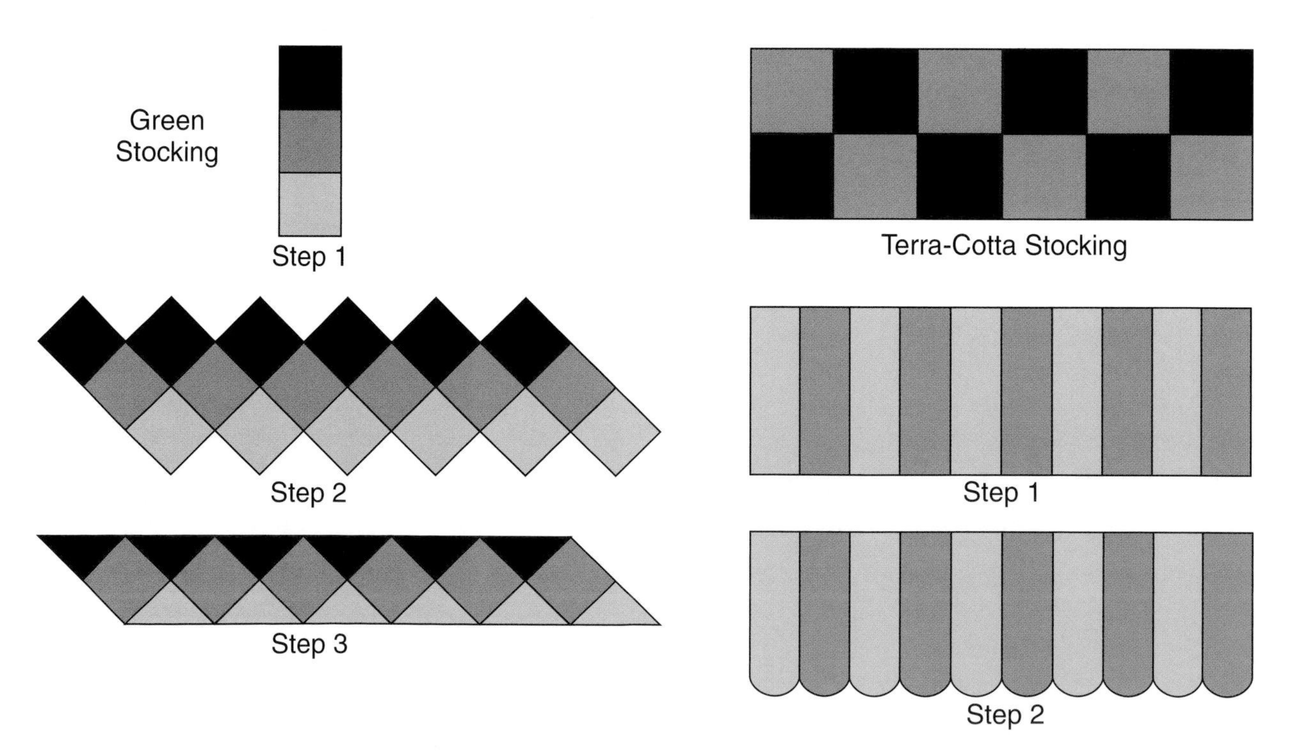

to the lining/border. Press the seam allowances open. Sew together the short edges of the pieced fabric with a ½-inch seam allowance, forming a circle. Press the seam allowances open; turn the cuff right side out. Fold the cuff in half, aligning the raw edges; press. Baste the top edges together.

Urn-Topper Wreath

Shown at right and on page 79.

YOU WILL NEED

- 18-inch twig wreath
- Boysenberry garland
- Evergreen bough
- Green florist's wire
- Wire cutters
- Five artificial grape bunches
- Bay leaf branches
- Glue gun and hotmelt adhesive
- Green planter's moss
- Reindeer moss
- Spanish moss
- Artificial quail

INSTRUCTIONS

Drape the boysenberry garland on the front of the twig wreath and position the evergreen bough at the top of the wreath. Wire the garland and bough to the wreath.

Arrange the grape bunches on the wreath. When pleased with the arrangement, wire the grapes in place.

Separate the bay leaf branches into smaller sections; hot glue the leaves around the wreath, filling in any open spaces and tucking the leaves between the grape bunches. Hot-glue small moss pieces around the wreath. Wire the quail to the evergreen bough.

Elegant Tree Skirt

Shown on page 94.

YOU WILL NEED

- 1 yard of red-print jacquard fabric
- ½ yard of green-print jacquard fabric
- ⅛ yard of curry gold embroidered fabric
- ⅜ yard of dark gold silk dupioni fabric
- Matching sewing threads
- Fabric-marking pencil

INSTRUCTIONS

Sew all pieces with right sides together using ¼-inch seam allowances, unless otherwise noted.

Cut the Fabric

From the red print jacquard fabric, cut one 34-inch square. From the green print jacquard fabric, cut four 3½×34-inch strips. From the curry gold

embroidered fabric, cut four 3½-inch squares. From the dark gold silk dupioni fabric, cut six 2×44-inch strips.

Sew the Tree Skirt

Sew a ½×34-inch green-print strip to the left and right edges of the 34-inch red-print square (see Illustration A *below left*). Zigzag-stitch or overcast the seam allowances together. Press the seam allowances toward the red-print square.

Sew a 3½-inch curry gold square to each end of the remaining 34-inch strips. Zigzag-stitch or overcast the seam allowances; press toward the curry gold squares.

Sew one pieced strip to the top of the 34-inch square and one to the bottom, matching the seams. Zigzag-stitch or overcast the seam allowances; press the seam allowances toward the red-print fabric square. (Refer to Illustration B *below center.*)

To find the center, fold the pieced tree skirt into quarters, creating a smaller square. Lightly press the folds to serve as placement guides; unfold and smooth out the fabric, wrong side up on a flat surface. For the tree trunk opening, use the fabric-marking pencil to draw a 6-inch diameter circle on the skirt back, centering the circle on the fabric where the creases intersect. For the center back opening, cut from the center to the outer edge along one of the creases. (Refer to Illustration C *below right.*)

For the binding, sew the short ends of the 2×44-inch strips together to make a continuous length. Press under ¼ inch on one long edge of the binding. Sew the remaining long edge of the binding to the center back and outside edges of the tree skirt, mitering the binding at the corners. Fold the binding to the wrong side of the tree skirt, covering the stitching line. Edgestitch the binding in place. Center and sew the remaining binding to the edges of the tree trunk opening in the same manner, creating ties with the excess binding at the center back opening.

All designs by Mary Jo Hiney

Pomegranate Wreath

Shown on pages 80 and 95.

YOU WILL NEED

- Grapevine wreath
- Green sheet moss
- Spanish moss
- Preserved solidago, mugwort, juniper, and annual purple statice

Illustration A

Illustration B

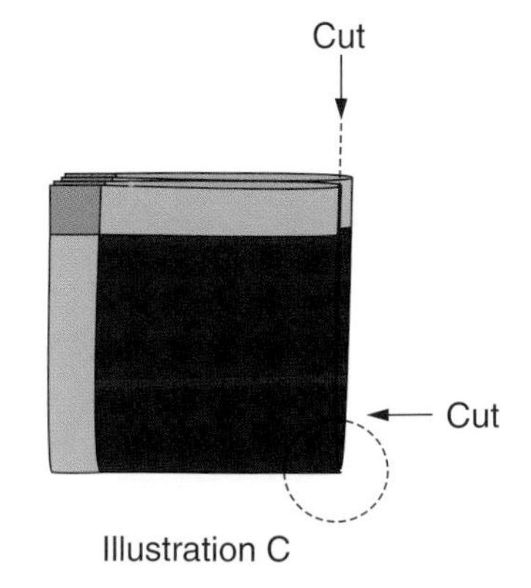

Illustration C

- Dried purple globe amaranth, rust celosia, cream celosia, tansy, yarrow, tallow berries, and safflower
- 12 fresh pomegranates of assorted sizes
- 16-gauge florist's wire
- Long dollmaking needle (one that will go through pomegranates)
- Glue gun and hotmelt adhesive

INSTRUCTIONS

Cover the top and sides of the grapevine wreath with green sheet moss. Hot-glue the sheet moss in place.

Push the needle through a pomegranate about a quarter of the way up from the bottom smooth side. Cut a 20-inch length of wire; thread the wire through the hole in the pomegranate. Center the pomegranate on the wire; twist the wire tails several times close to the base of the pomegranate, leaving the tails loose to secure the pomegranate to the wreath later. Wire all the pomegranates in this same manner. Referring to the photograph *at right*, hot-glue and firmly wire four groupings of three pomegranates around the wreath. Fill in around and between the pomegranates with Spanish moss.

Trim the dried and preserved materials into 3- to 4-inch lengths. Hot-glue small clumps of the dried and preserved materials around the wreath until you are pleased with the arrangement.

Secure a length of wire to the back of the wreath as a hanger. The wreath will be fairly heavy so you may need to double or triple the wire. As the pomegranates dry out, fill in around them with more moss or extra dried floral materials.

Wreath designed by Howell Tree Farm

DECORATING WITH FRESH POMEGRANATES

Decorating with fresh pomegranates is one of the hottest holiday trends. Florists use them throughout the holiday season in wreaths, floral arrangements, swags, and tablescapes.

Pomegranates are for sale August through December with their peak availability in October and November—just in time to create fabulous decorations for your holiday decor. When planning your decorations, select fresh pomegranates that are firm and round with a deep red color. Store them in a cool place until you are ready to use them.

To make the fruit brighter and shinier, apply a light coat of cooking oil to the surface. Remove the excess with a paper towel, buffing the surface until it shines.

A great way to create extra sparkle in your decoration without losing the rich red color of the pomegranate is to dust the surface of a pomegranate with an aerosol spray glitter from your crafts store. Don't try this is you've previously shined the surface, the glitter won't stick.

Attach pomegranates to swags in the same manner as for a wreath, by wiring the base of the pomegranate with florist's wire. To use the fruits in floral arrangements, insert two bamboo (cooking) skewers 1 inch deep and 1 inch apart in the base of each pomegranate. Place the skewers into the florist's foam inside the container.

Ellen

Creative Cards and Gift Wrap

WHEN PRESENTATION IS EVERYTHING, pull out all your paper-crafting stops and fashion the kinds of cards and gift wraps that can't be bought in any store.

A party table wouldn't be well-dressed without place cards to summon family or friends to their chairs. The pieces for the frosty fellow *opposite* fasten in place with paper brads.

Folded squares of paper promise a memorable gathering when they're decorated with gleaming holiday motifs, *above*.

Don't toss out your extra handmade cards after Christmas. Pop a favorite card into a frame to display on a table or on a beckoning wall space.

Fans of romantic styling will love these pleated paper cards *above*. Reminiscent of antique calling cards, they're worked with crafts knives and deckle-edged scissors and incorporate elegant stickers, buttons, and sparkling cording.

Pick a theme and a paper scheme; then treat your family and friends to one of these handmade expressions. More than greeting cards, these three designs *left* unfold as small treasures—handmade gifts from the heart—to be saved and enjoyed long after the season is done. The fanciful ladybug, dragonfly, and butterfly evolve as winged Christmas creatures, cut from seasonal papers and colors.

Even materials as common as brown paper and string can take a pretty turn as gift bags and package wraps, *above*. These get a fancy addressing with faux sticker stamps (or pretty canceled ones you've collected), colored circle tags, rubber stamps, and "routing" labels that go to work as gift tags.

If you don't have enough of any one paper to completely cover a box, layer it! The striking cover-ups *opposite* make resourceful use of paper leftovers. For holiday flavor, scatter snowflake and holly punch-outs all over.

Christmas Tree Place Card

Shown opposite and on page 97.

YOU WILL NEED

- Tracing paper
- 4×5½-inch rectangle of white card stock
- Metallic gold, green, and red card stock
- Dimensional adhesive (we used JudiKins Diamond Glaze)
- Adhesive foam dot
- Black fine-tip permanent marking pen

INSTRUCTIONS

Trace the tree patterns *opposite* onto tracing paper. Cut out each pattern piece. Trace each pattern once on the wrong side of the metallic green card stock, or the metallic red card stock. Cut out all the card stock pieces. Cut a small tree trunk from the metallic gold card stock.

For the place card, fold the 4×5½-inch rectangle of white card stock in half to measure 4×2¾ inches. Use dimensional adhesive to glue the red tree pieces behind the corresponding green pieces, extending the red about ¹⁄16 inch below the green. Glue the middle triangle to the top two-thirds of the bottom triangle. Glue the top triangle to the top half of the middle triangle. Glue the trunk to the center bottom on the tree back. Mount the tree on the place card with an adhesive dot. Personalize the place card using the black permanent marking pen.

Poinsettia Place Card

Shown opposite and on page 97.

YOU WILL NEED

- Tracing paper
- 4×5½-inch rectangle of pale green parchment paper
- Metallic gold, green, and red card stock
- ¼-inch hole punch
- Dimensional adhesive (we used JudiKins Diamond Glaze)
- Adhesive foam dots
- Black fine-tip permanent marking pen

INSTRUCTIONS

Trace the patterns *opposite* onto tracing paper. Cut out the pattern pieces. Trace the petals pattern once on the wrong side of the metallic red card stock. Trace the leaves pattern once on the wrong side of the metallic green card stock. Cut out the card stock pieces. For the flower center, punch three circles from metallic gold card stock with the hole punch.

For the place card, fold the 4×5½-inch rectangle of pale green parchment paper in half to measure 4×2¾ inches. Use dimensional adhesive to glue the green leaf piece behind the red petal piece. Glue the gold circles to the center of the petal piece. Mount the poinsettia on the place card with an adhesive dot. Personalize the place card using the black permanent marking pen.

Snowy Tree Place Card

Shown on page 97.

YOU WILL NEED

- 4×6½-inch rectangle of white card stock
- Metallic gold, green, and red card stock
- Ruler
- Scoring tool
- ⅛-inch hole punch
- Double-stick tape
- Gold gel pen

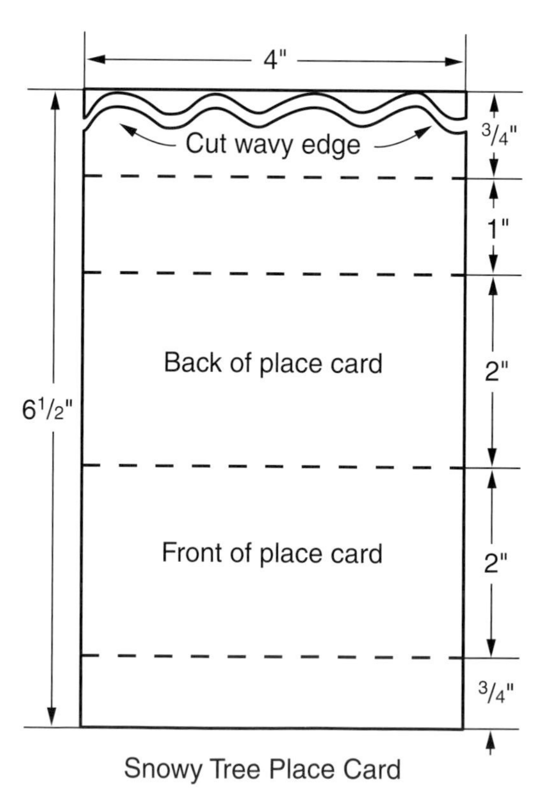

Snowy Tree Place Card

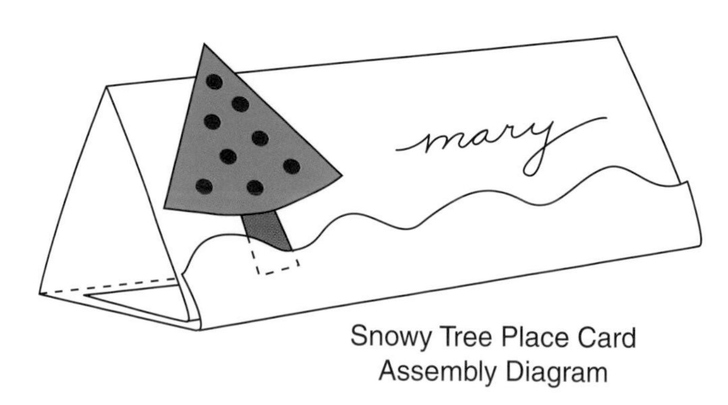

Snowy Tree Place Card
Assembly Diagram

INSTRUCTIONS

Mark the fold lines at both long edges of the 4×6½-inch rectangle of white card stock, referring to the diagram *opposite*. Use a ruler to connect each set of pencil marks and score the lines. Fold the rectangle along the score lines, creating a tent shape with a ¾-inch flap at the bottom front. For the snow, cut waves into the front flap.

Trace the tree and trunk patterns *below* onto tracing paper. Trace the tree onto the back of a piece of metallic green card stock. Trace the tree onto the back of a piece of metallic red card stock. Randomly punch holes in the green tree piece using the ⅛-inch hole punch. Use tiny pieces of double-stick tape to attach the red tree to the center of the green tree. Cut a tree trunk from the metallic gold card stock. Glue the trunk to the center bottom on the tree back. Mount the tree on the place card with double-stick tape. Personalize the place card with the gold gel pen. Use double-stick tape to fasten the bottom and front flaps of the place card, creating the tent shape (see the diagram *opposite*).

Snowman Place Card

Shown on pages 96 and 104.

YOU WILL NEED

- Tracing paper
- Card stock: 5⅜×6⅛-inch rectangle each of black, and white, red, green, brown, and orange
- Ruler
- Scoring tool
- Glue stick
- 1⁄16-inch hole punch
- Black permanent marking pen (we used 08 Pigma Micron)
- Transparent tape
- Nine 8-millimeter brass paper fasteners

INSTRUCTIONS

Mark the fold lines at both long edges of the 5⅜x6 ⅛-inch rectangle of black card stock, referring to the diagram on *page 104*. Use a ruler to connect each set of pencil marks and score the lines. Fold the rectangle along the score lines, creating an irregular M-shape.

From the white card stock, cut a 1x5⅜-inch strip for the snow, cutting one long edge wavy. Mount the snow on the front of the place card with the glue stick.

Trace the snowman and the tree patterns on *page 105* onto tracing paper. Cut out each pattern piece. Referring to the photographs on *pages 96 and 104*, trace the patterns onto the appropriate color of card stock. Cut out all the card stock pieces and punch holes in the pieces as marked on the patterns. Punch three holes in the black piece as indicated in the assembly diagram.

Use the black marker to personalize the sign and to draw the eyes, mouth, and buttons on the snowman pieces. For the nose, cut a tiny slit in the face centered below the eyes. Working from

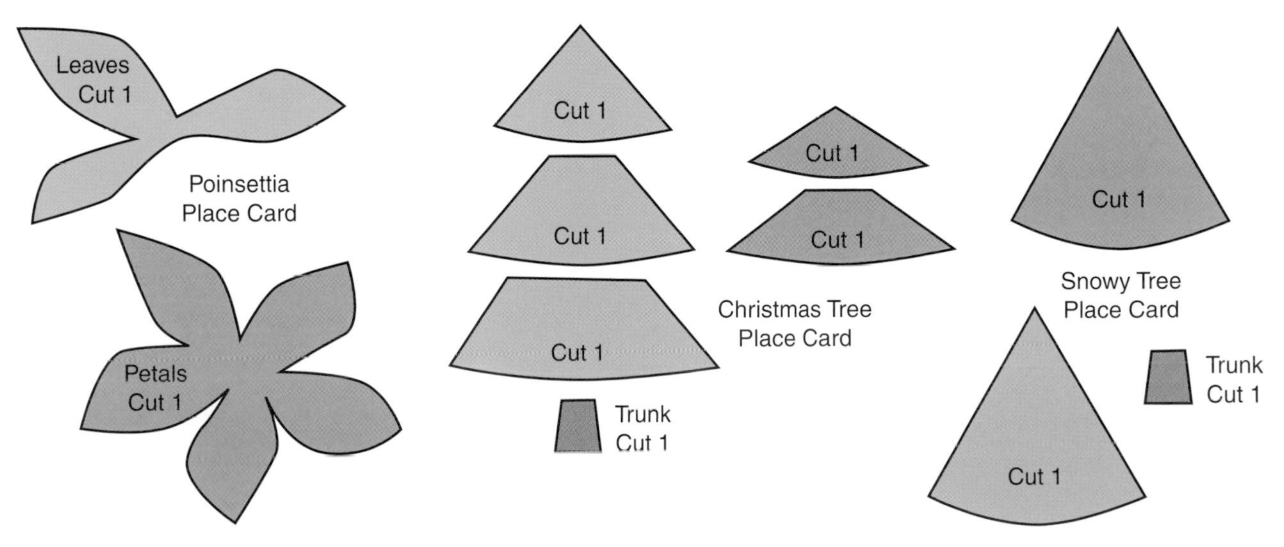

back to front, insert the narrow pointed end of the nose through the slit. Tape the wide end of the nose on the back. Overlap the pieces, matching the holes. To connect the pieces, place paper fasteners through the holes and flatten the ends on the back. Position the sign, snowman, and tree.

Holiday Bug Cards

Shown on pages 98 and 106.

YOU WILL NEED

For each card:
- Tracing paper
- Scissors
- Transparent tape
- Double-stick tape
- Dimensional adhesive (we used JudiKins Diamond Glaze)

For the Ladybug Card:
- 5½x8½-inch piece of green card stock
- 5¼x4-inch piece of white card stock
- Scraps of black, green, and red card stock
- Black text-weight paper
- 3⁄16-inch hole punch
- Spiral punch
- Black permanent marking pen (we used 01 Pigma Micron)
- 'Tis the Season rubber stamp by Stampin' Up
- Black ink pad

For the Dragonfly Card:
- 8½x5½-inch piece of green parchment card stock
- 3¾x5-inch piece of plaid-patterned scrapbook paper
- 2¾x4-inch piece of white text-weight paper
- Green and red card stock
- Wavy-edge paper scissors
- Vellum
- ⅛-inch hole punch

For the Butterfly Card:
- 8½x5½-inch piece of white card stock
- 3¾x2½-inch piece of white card stock
- 5¼x4-inch piece of green-with-white-stars scrapbook paper
- Metallic gold kraft wrapping paper
- Red text-weight paper
- Green card stock
- Deckle-edge paper scissors
- Small diamond punch
- Spiral punch

INSTRUCTIONS

Ladybug Card: Fold the green card stock in half to measure 5½x4¼ inches. Cut a 5¼x4-inch piece of white card stock; center and glue it to the front of the green card stock.

To make the ladybug, first trace the ladybug body and shell patterns on *page 107*, and transfer them to red and black card stock. Cut out the pieces from the card stock. Cut three ⅛x1½-inch-long strips of black card stock for the legs. Punch two spirals from black paper for the feelers. Punch six dots

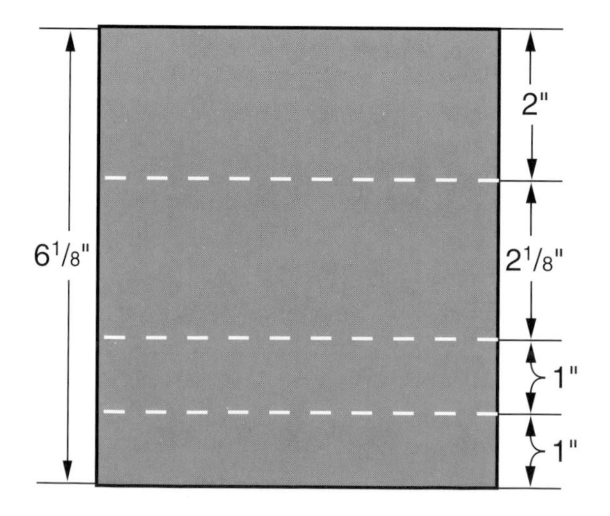

Snowman Place Card Assembly Diagram

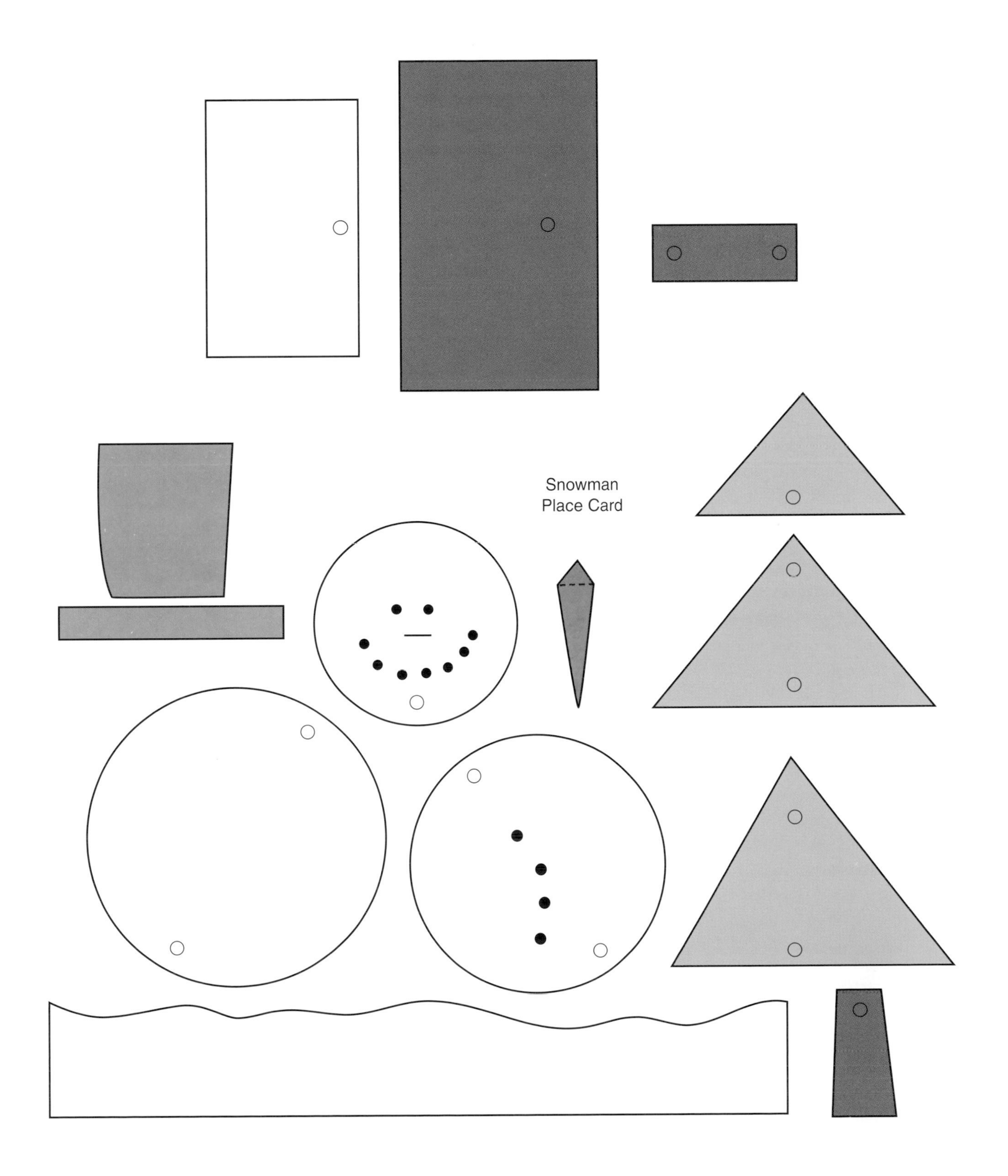
Snowman
Place Card

from the green card stock with the hole punch. Glue the red shell on top of the black body piece. Arrange the three black leg strips, crossed on the underside of the black body piece, and tape them in place. With dimensional adhesive, adhere the two black feelers under the ladybug head and the six green circles on top of the red shell.

Stamp " 'Tis the season" on the front lower third of the card with black ink. Adhere the ladybug to the card about 1 inch away from the stamped words with double-stick tape. Use the black marking pen to make a squiggly dotted line starting at the end of "season" to the bottom of the bug.

Dragonfly Card: Fold the green parchment card stock in half to measure 5½x4¼ inches. Cut a wavy edge along all four sides of the plaid paper with wavy-edge scissors. Cut a 1¾x3⅛-inch window out of the center of this paper, again making the edges wavy. Cut a 1⅝x3-inch window with wavy edges out of the center of the white paper. Center and attach the white paper behind the plaid paper with double-stick tape so there is an even ⅛-inch margin between the two windows. Center and adhere the plaid paper to the front of the parchment card with double-stick tape.

Trace the dragonfly's body pattern on *page 107*, and transfer it to the green card stock. Punch two ⅛-inch dots from red card stock, and glue them to the top of the dragonfly's head with dimensional adhesive. Trace and transfer the wings pattern onto folded vellum. Cut out the wings. Adhere them to the body as shown in the photo *below*.

Cut a narrow strip of double-stick tape, place it under the dragonfly's body, and adhere it to the front of the card. Cut four squares of double-stick tape small enough so that each one will fit under the tip of each wing. Apply the tape to the tip of each wing. Press down on each wing tip to hold them in place on the card.

Butterfly Card: Fold the larger piece of white card stock in half to measure 5½x4¼ inches. Use double-stick tape to attach all the layers to the card. Center and attach the green scrapbook paper to the front of the white card. Using deckle-edge scissors, cut a 4⅛x3-inch rectangle from the gold kraft paper; center and adhere it to the front of the card. Center and adhere the smaller piece of white card stock to the front of the card.

Trace the butterfly body/wing and body center patterns on *page 107*. Transfer one body/wing pattern to green card stock and one body/wing pattern to the red paper; cut them out. Transfer the body center pattern to red card stock; cut it out. Trim 1/16 inch around from the red body/wing piece. Referring to the photo *below*, punch a design in each wing tip using the diamond punch. Use dimensional adhesive to attach the red body center to the top of the body/wing piece.

Adhere the red body/wing piece to the underside of the green body/wing piece. For the feelers, punch two spirals from the gold kraft paper; trim one end off each feeler as shown in the diagram on *page 107* and attach them to the underside of the body center with dimensional adhesive. Adhere the assembled butterfly to the front of the card with double-stick tape.

Layered Gift Wrap

Shown on page 101.

YOU WILL NEED

For each gift box:
- Adhesive spray mount
- Transparent tape
- Double-stick tape

For Holly-Banded Gift Wrap:
- Green-solid and red-patterned gift wrapping paper
- Gold paper
- Scallop-edge paper scissors
- Holly leaves punch
- Red ¼-inch dot stickers

For Snowflake Gift Wrap:
- Green-solid and gold-solid gift-wrapping papers
- Snowflake punch

For the Burgundy-and-Gold Gift Wrap:
- Burgundy-solid and gold-pattered gift-wrapping papers
- Gold ribbon
- Gold cording
- Gold metallic marking pen

For the Gift Bag:
- Paper sack
- Green-patterned and gold-solid gift-wrapping papers
- ¼-inch hole punch
- 24 inches of ½-inch-wide gold ribbon

INSTRUCTIONS

Holly Banded Gift Wrap: Wrap the entire box with green-solid wrapping paper. Cut a piece of red-patterned wrapping paper to cover about one-third of the box. Apply lengths of double-stick tape along the bottom edge on the back of the red-patterned paper. Wrap one end of the box with the red-patterned paper.

For the holly band, use the scallop-edge paper scissors to cut a 1¾-inch-wide strip from the gold paper long enough to wrap around the box. Position the strip on the box and punch holly leaves in the strip for the box front. Wrap the band around the box and secure the ends with double-stick tape. Stick a red dot on the holly band, under the bottom leaf of each punched holly leaf.

Snowflake Gift Wrap: Wrap the entire box with gold wrapping paper. Cut a piece of green wrapping paper to cover about the top one-third of the box, curving the bottom edge. Punch snowflakes in the green paper that will be on the box sides; reserve the snowflakes. Apply adhesive spray mount to the back of the green wrapping paper. Wrap the box top with the green paper, using double-stick tape to secure the paper at the center top of the box. Glue the punched snowflakes onto the gold paper. Add a bow as desired.

Burgundy-and-Gold Gift Wrap: Wrap the entire box in burgundy wrapping paper. Cut a piece of gold wrapping paper to cover about the top one-third of the box. If the pattern of the gold paper is swirled or curved as shown for our sample on *page 101*, cut the bottom edge to incorporate the swirled design of the paper. Then apply spray adhesive to the back of the gold wrapping paper, and attach the gold paper to the top of the box.

If desired, make a matching gift tag from a rectangle of burgundy paper. Cut a piece of gold wrapping paper for the seal. Use double-stick tape to attach the seal to one edge of the burgundy rectangle, sandwiching the end of a length of gold cording between the two pieces of paper. Write a message on the burgundy paper using a metallic gold marking pen. Encircle the package once with ribbon, and tie on a gold ribbon bow. Tie the gift tag at the base of the bow.

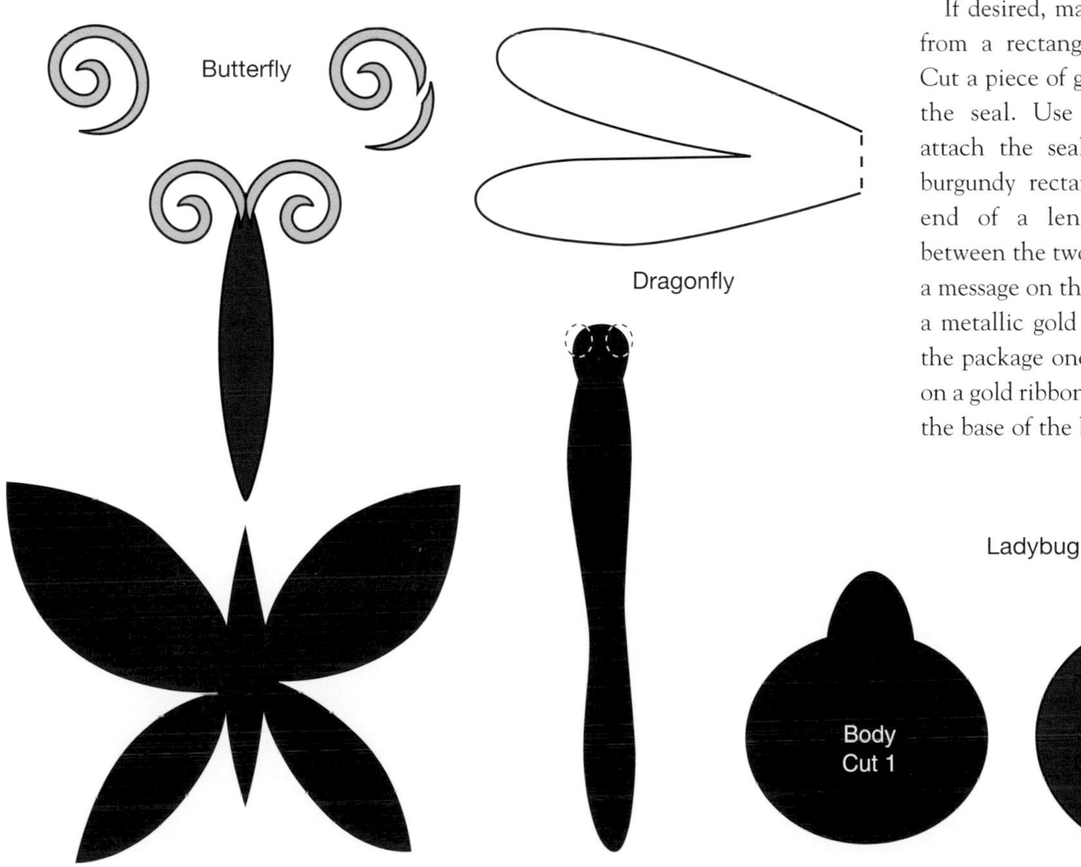

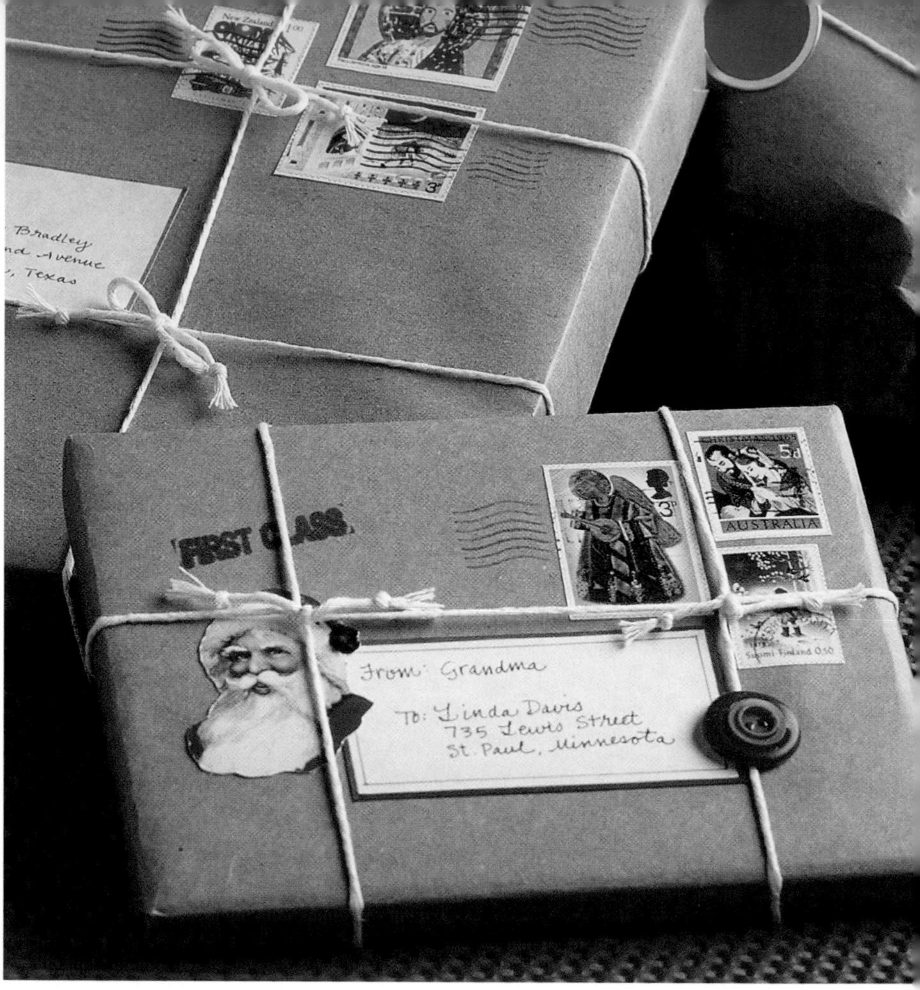

Gift Bag: Apply adhesive spray mount to the back of the green-patterned wrapping paper, and cover the entire front and bottom of the paper bag. Cut a rectangle of gold gift wrapping paper that is two-thirds the height of the paper bag, curved on the bottom, and about 2 inches taller than the sack. Apply adhesive spray mount to the back of the gold paper. Cover the top portion of the bag, folding the top 2 inches of gold paper over the top edge. Punch two holes evenly spaced on the front and back of the bag..

Cut two 12-inch pieces of ribbon. Thread the tails of one ribbon through the holes in one side of the bag. Tie each end of the ribbon into a knot. Repeat for the other side.

Old-Fashioned Packages

Shown at right and on page 100.

YOU WILL NEED

- Brown kraft paper or gift bag
- Tan-and-white checked scrapbook paper
- Parchment paper
- Shipping tag for gift bag
- Glue stick
- Fine-tip permanent markers
- Antique reproduction stickers
- Colorful cancelled holiday postage stamps
- Assorted postal rubber stamps
- Black ink pad
- Old buttons
- Dimensional adhesive (we used JudiKins Diamond Glaze)
- Kitchen twine
- $1\frac{1}{4}$-inch-diameter round key tags
- Glue gun and red hotmelt adhesive stick
- Transparent tape

INSTRUCTIONS

Note: *Refer to the photograph on page 100 for more ideas on wrapping old-fashioned packages.*

Wrap the gift box with brown kraft paper, or place the gift in a brown paper gift bag. For a gift tag, cut a rectangle from the parchment paper. If desired, cut a piece of scrapbook paper slightly larger than the parchment paper. Layer the papers with the glue stick. Use the markers to add borders. Write the recipient's and the giver's names on the gift tag or a shipping tag.

To decorate the tags, use stickers, rubber stamps and the black ink pad, or attach buttons with the dimensional adhesive. Attach the label to the gift with glue, or knot the shipping tag string around the bag's handle.

Embellish the package with more stickers, colorful cancelled holiday stamps, and stamped images. Tie kitchen twine around the packages, attaching key tags and buttons to the twine. For a "wax seal," place a red hotmelt adhesive stick in the glue gun. Squeeze out a round blob of red hotmelt adhesive on the package, and over a twine tie. Immediately press a button into the adhesive.

Old-Fashioned Cards

Shown opposite and on page 99.

YOU WILL NEED

For each card:

- $4\frac{1}{4} \times 8\frac{1}{2}$-inch piece of red or green card stock
- Crafts knife, metal straightedge, and cutting mat
- Scoring tool
- Antique reproduction stickers
- White vellum
- Deckle-edged scissors
- Double-stick tape
- Dimensional adhesive (we used JudiKins Diamond Glaze)

For the red card:
- Holly border stickers
- Metallic silver thread
- Assorted small buttons

For the green card:
- Gold foil card stock
- Ivory-and-gold scrapbooking border
- Metallic gold cord

INSTRUCTIONS

Mark the cutting and fold lines on the red or green card stock, referring to the diagram *below*. Use the straightedge and crafts knife to cut along the solid lines. Very lightly score the dotted fold lines. Fold the card along the score lines, making crisp creases.

Red Card: Apply holly border stickers and a horizontal rectangle sticker to the card, referring to the photograph at *left* for placement. Apply a vertical rectangle sticker to the vellum. Use the deckle-edged scissors to cut around the vellum, creating a 1/8-inch border. Mount the vellum on the card with double-stick tape. Tie a bow with metallic silver thread. Glue the bow and buttons to the card with dimensional adhesive.

Green Card: Apply a horizontal rectangle sticker to the vellum. Use the deckle-edged scissors to cut around the vellum, creating a 1/8-inch border. Mount the vellum on the gold foil card stock. Cut the gold card stock 1/8 inch beyond the edges of the vellum. Mount the gold card stock on the card with double-stick tape, referring to the photograph on *page 99* for placement. Use double-stick tape to mount the ivory-and-gold border. Tie a bow with gold cord, and glue it to the center of the border with dimensional adhesive.

All designs by Jean Wilson

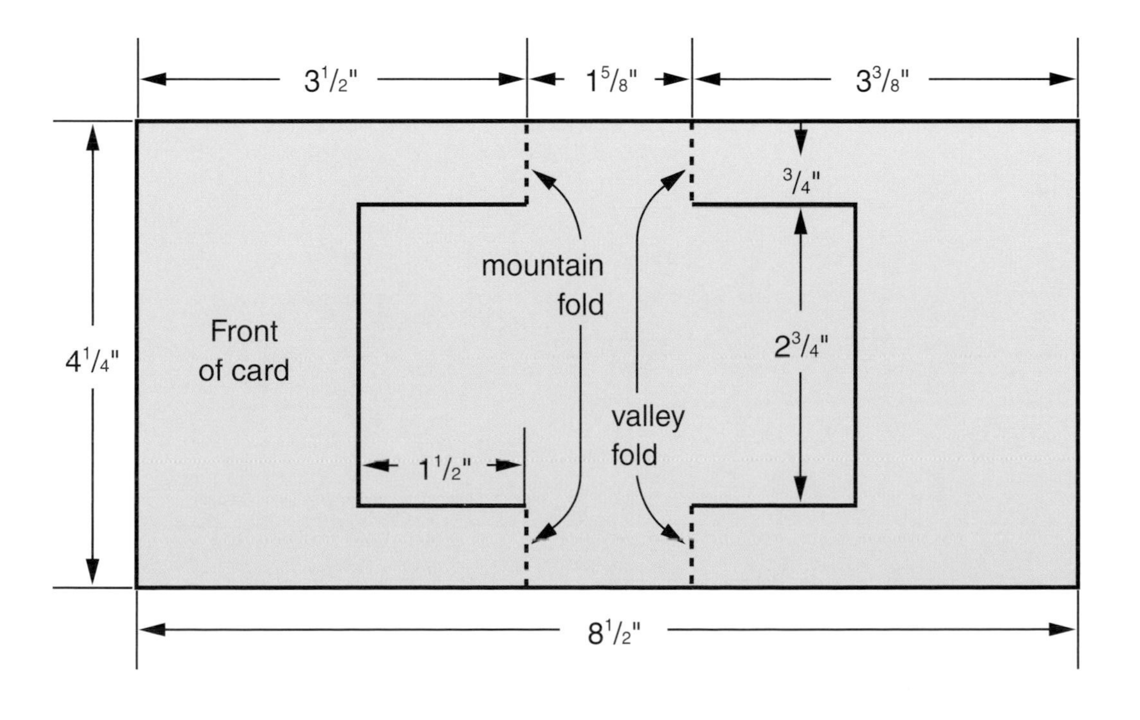

Happy

Gifts for Giving

TAKING THE TIME TO MAKE A GIFT as special as the recipient makes holiday gift giving all the more enjoyable. Whether you start weeks before Christmas or need something in a twinkling, you'll find the perfect idea in this collection.

Stockings are always a favorite choice for holding holiday surprises, but these perky miniatures *opposite* are a gift in themselves. Choose from knitted stripes or funky polka dots. Or create the whimsical paper stocking shown on *page 126*.

Even the person who has "everything" will be happy to receive a lavish towel set, *above,* that has been personalized to coordinate with the bathroom. Attach fabric bands to purchased towels; then add machine-embroidered details, trims, and contrasting ribbon embellishments to make a gift that's sure to please.

Give the cozy crocheted comforter at *right,* and the happy recipient is sure to appreciate your hard work—especially when there's a chill in the air. Men and women alike will find the diamond design appealing for most any decorating scheme.

Christmas Wonder
Christmas Wishes
Christmas Blessings
Christmas Memories
Let it snow!

Make time fly on subzero afternoons or during long car rides to Grandma's with a felt patchwork checkerboard that includes baked-clay peppermint-swirl checkers, *above*. When the game is over, simply fold the board in thirds, store the game pieces inside the snap pocket, and close it with a rickrack tie.

Christmas cards, photos, or other holiday mementos find a home inside a wooden box featuring a whimsical needlework design stitched on the lid, *opposite*. Simple stitches sewn over a traced image make the work quick and easy to complete.

A girl can never have too many purses. The pretty posy bag *above* is just the right size when a small amount of money and a few cosmetic essentials are all you need to take along. Hand-stitch the petite bag using felt, pearl cotton, and beads.

Carefully stitched with satin brocade and silk lining fabrics, the envelope bag *opposite* makes a pretty holder for a journal or a sentimental book of poems. Unfold a paper envelope and trace the shape to make your own pattern for the bag.

Pretty Posy Bag

Shown on page 116.

YOU WILL NEED

- Tracing paper
- National NonWovens felt: Island Storm, Grandma's Garnet, English Rose, Mellow Yellow, Loden, and Grassy Meadows
- Pinking shears
- DMC pearl cotton: #8—true mauve (3687), dark garnet (814), dark yellow (742), and true pistachio (320); #5 light navy (334)
- Embroidery needle
- Mill Hill beads: frosted royal plum (62012) and medium nutmeg bugle (82053)
- Sewing thread to match beads
- 18-inch length of 3/16-inch-diameter pale rose twisted cording

INSTRUCTIONS

Trace the patterns *below* onto tracing paper. Cut out the pattern pieces.

From Island Storm felt, cut one 6×9-inch rectangle for the bag back/top flap and one 6-inch square for the bag front. From Grandma's Garnet felt, cut one rose. From English Rose felt, cut one rose center and one of each daisy center, using the pinking shears to cut the daisy centers. From the Mellow Yellow felt, cut one daisy. From the Loden felt, cut two large leaves and one small leaf. From the Grassy Meadows felt, cut two large leaves and one small leaf. If desired, cut one heart from English Rose felt for the back of the bag.

Position the bag front on the bag back/top flap, aligning the bottom and side edges. Round the bottom corners of the bag, cutting through both layers and rounding the corners of the flap. Refer to the illustration *opposite* to position the daisy, rose, and leaf felt shapes on the 3-inch wide top flap and as a guide for embroidery. Pin the shapes in place and stitch in the order that follows.

Position the leaves on the flap. Use green pearl cotton to blanket-stitch all edges of the leaves, sewing them to the flap. Pin the daisy and the rose in place, overlapping the leaves. Use yellow pearl cotton to sew running stitches close to the edges of the daisy and garnet pearl cotton to blanket-stitch along all edges of the rose, sewing them to the flap.

Make several small cuts in each daisy center shape, cutting from the

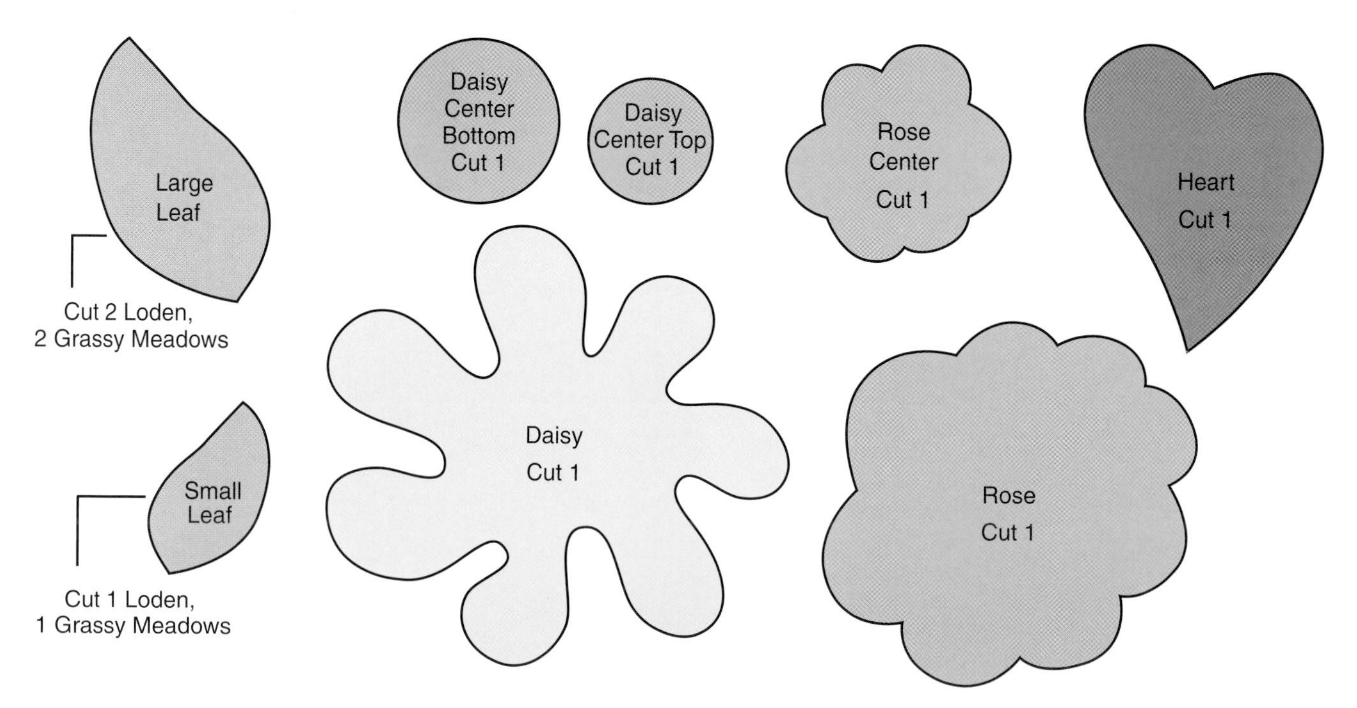

outer edge toward the center. Layer the daisy centers and place them on the daisy. Sew the centers in place with six seed beads and matching sewing thread. Sew a bugle bead to each daisy petal. Pin the rose center on the rose; blanket-stitch in place with rose pearl cotton. Randomly sew seed beads on the rose center with matching sewing thread.

Use a double length of green pearl cotton to stem-stitch a curved tendril from each flower. Sew seed beads along the right tendril.

Blanket-stitch along the top edge of the bag front with blue pearl cotton. With wrong sides facing, pin the bag front to the back, aligning the side and bottom edges. Use blue pearl cotton to blanket-stitch the side and bottom edges together. Working from the right side of the flap, blanket-stitch along the edges of the flap.

For the bag strap, sew the ends of the twisted cording to the inside top corners of the bag.

Designed by Robin Kingsley

Envelope Bag

Shown on pages 117 and 120.

YOU WILL NEED

Note: The envelope bag shown measures 12×9 inches and uses 5/8 yard each of satin brocade and silk lining fabric and 1½ yards of ribbon.
Envelope
Graph paper
Multicolor satin brocade
Silk lining fabric
½-inch-wide sheer lavender ribbon
Matching sewing thread

INSTRUCTIONS

To make the pattern, completely unfold an existing envelope. Enlarge the envelope on graph paper to the size you want; add ½-inch seam allowances to all edges. Cut out the pattern piece.

Use the pattern to cut one matching shape from both the satin brocade and the silk lining fabrics. For the ribbon ties, fold over one-third of the ribbon. Bunch up and pin the fold on the right side of the brocade shape, positioning it on the tip of the envelope's top flap with the ribbon tails toward the center of the envelope. With right sides facing, pin the lining to the brocade envelope. Sew the brocade envelope to the lining, catching the ribbon fold in the stitching and leaving a 3 inch opening on one edge of the bottom flap for turning. Trim the seams and clip the curves. Turn the envelope right side out and press.

Fold in the side flaps and press, creating a strong crease at the left and right edges of the envelope. Fold up

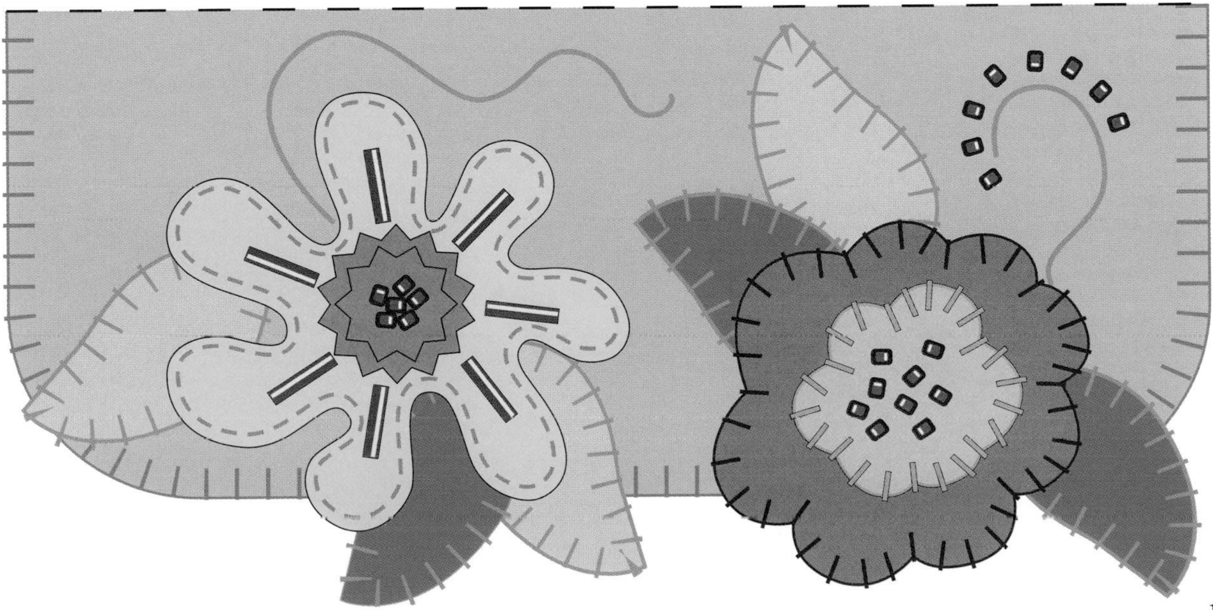

the bottom flap to overlap the bottom edges of the side flaps; press. Pin together the overlapped areas. Sew the overlapped areas together along the edges of the bottom flap, sewing as far as possible into the bottom corners of the envelope. Slip-stitch the remaining portion of the seam closed.

Insert a journal, book, or other gift item into the bag. Fold the top flap down, wrap the longer ribbon tail around the envelope, and tie the ribbon ends together.

Designed by Mary Jo Hiney

Travel Checkerboard and Checkers

Shown on pages 115 and 121.

YOU WILL NEED

- Felt: 3/8 yard of red, 1×49-inch strip of white, three squares of Christmas green, and one square each of three shades of green (dark, medium, and light)
- Red sewing thread
- Package of red medium rickrack
- Two red snaps
- Erasable fabric marker
- Waxed paper
- Sculpey III polymer clay: green, red, and white
- Sharp knife
- Baking sheet
- Baking parchment paper

INSTRUCTIONS

From the red felt, cut two 12-inch squares for the checkerboard front and back and four 2½×4-inch rectangles for the pocket flaps. From the Christmas green felt, cut one 3½×11-inch rectangle for the pockets and eleven 1½-inch squares for the checks. From one of the three remaining green felts, cut seven 1½-inch squares; from another green felt, cut five 1½-inch squares for the checks. Cut nine 1½-inch squares from the last piece of green felt for the squares.

Place one 12-inch red felt square on a flat surface for the checkerboard front. Place the 1½-inch green squares on the red square in a checkerboard pattern, arranging the green shades randomly; pin in place. Use red thread to sew the green squares to the red checkerboard front, sewing diagonally from corner to corner.

Sew the red rickrack along one long edge of the white felt strip with the outer edge of the rickrack just inside the cut edge of the felt. Pin the white felt strip to the wrong side of the checkerboard front, positioning it with one-half of the rickrack showing on the right side of the checkerboard and mitering the corners.

Pin the 2½×4-inch pocket flaps together in pairs. Sew ⅛ inch from the short edges and one long edge, sewing diagonally across the corners to shape the pockets. Trim the felt at the corners ⅛ inch beyond the diagonal stitching. Apply the top half of a snap to each pocket flap about ¼ inch from the center of the long stitched edge.

To mark the snaps, center the 3½×11-inch green pocket strip on the remaining 12-inch red felt square for the checkerboard back. Position a pocket flap at the open end of each pocket, aligning the outer edge of the flap with the checkerboard back. Mark the snap location on each end of the pocket strip with the erasable fabric marker. Apply the bottom half of a snap at each mark.

Reposition the green pocket strip on the red checkerboard back. Sew the pocket strip to the red back close to each long edge and across the center, creating two pockets. Reposition a pocket flap at the open end of each pocket; then sew ⅛-inch from the outer edge.

With wrong sides together, center the checkerboard front on the back. For the ties, fold the remaining rickrack in half and slip the fold between the front and back at the center of one of the nonpocket edges.

Sew the front to the back, catching the rickrack ties in the stitching.

To make the checkers, cover your work area with a sheet of waxed paper. Knead the clay between the palms of your hands until it is soft and pliable.

Roll 1-inch-diameter, 4-inch-long logs of green, red, and white clay. Cut each log lengthwise into quarters and then cut each quarter in half, creating eight triangle-shape wedges. Reassemble the wedges to make two striped logs, alternating four red wedges with four white and four green wedges with four white. Firmly press the wedges together for each log. Cut twelve 3⁄16-inch-wide slices from the logs for the checkers.

Place the checkers on a baking sheet covered with baking parchment paper. Put the baking sheet in the oven and bake the checkers according to the instructions on the clay package.

When the checkers are cool, store the green peppermints in one pocket and the red in the other. Roll up the checkerboard and tie the rickrack.

Designed by Mary Jo Hiney

Christmas Wishes Box

Shown on page 114.

YOU WILL NEED

- Tracing paper
- Permanent marking pen
- Fabric marking pen or pencil
- 12×12-inch piece of ivory cotton fabric or muslin
- DMC embroidery floss as listed in the color key
- Embroidery needle
- Embroidery hoop
- Oak needlework box with a 6×6-inch design area

INSTRUCTIONS

Trace the design on *page 123* with a permanent marking pen onto tracing paper. Tape the traced design to a sunny window; center and tape the fabric over the traced design. Using a fabric marking pen or pencil, lightly trace the design onto the fabric.

Place the fabric in an embroidery hoop to work. Then, using one ply of the embroidery floss and following the color key for the floss colors, embroider the design. Make French knots as indicated by the dots on the pattern. Work cross-stitches for the Xes and satin stitches for the solid areas. Work the outlines for the boxed sections in running stitches, and use straight stitches for the bushes by the bottom right house. Work backstitches for the lettering, the stars, and all remaining design areas.

If necessary, launder the stitchery to remove the pattern markings. Press the finished stitchery from the back. Mount it into the lid of the box, following manufacturer's instructions.

Designed by Gail Bussi

Crocheted Christmas Comforter

Shown on pages 113 and 125.

Skill Level: Beginner

Finished size: $42\frac{1}{2}\times52\frac{1}{2}$ inches

YOU WILL NEED

Lion Brand Homespun yarn (Art. 790) 98% acrylic, 2% polyester, 6 ounces (171 grams); 185 yds. (169 meters); chunky weight yarns
3 skeins #329 Waterfall (A)
4 skeins #303 Deco (B)
Size K crochet hook or size needed to obtain gauge
Blunt end tapestry needle

Gauge: 10 sc and 10 rows = 4 inches

Abbreviations Used
Chain = ch
Loop = lp
Single crochet = sc
Slip stitch = sl st
Stitch = st
Yarn over = yo

Note: *To change color, work last st with color in use until last yo. Drop yarn in use and with new yarn color, complete the stitch.*

INSTRUCTIONS

Block (make 12): With A, ch 28.
Row 1: Sc in second ch from hook and in each of next 25 ch. Insert hook in last ch and draw up a lp (2 lps on hook). Drop A and with B (slip knot on hook), draw knot lp through the 2 lps on the hook—color change made. With B, ch 1, turn.

continued on page 124

Christmas Wishes Box Key

DMC

501	/	Dark blue-green—writing
502	/	Medium blue-green—Christmas tree branches, holly bush
3831	/	Dark raspberry—red lines, snowman hearts
3832	/	Medium raspberry—chimney, snowman buttons, big Christmas tree garland
729	/	Medium old gold—big stars, moon
676	/	Light old gold—small stars
922	/	Light copper—snowman nose
414	/	Dark steel—snowman body and head, bottom house roof
415	/	Light pearl gray—houses base
535	/	True ash gray—window bars, snowman mouth
931	/	Medium antique blue—snowman hat band, top of door on bottom house, chimney top
932	/	True antique blue—top house window shutters, bottom house window box, snowman vest, body of hat
3790	/	Deep beige-gray—tree trunks, top house roof and door, snowman arms
612	/	Medium drab brown—top house walls, big tree pot, bottom house door
642	/	Medium beige-gray—bottom house walls
3782	/	Light mocha—top house window box

FRENCH KNOTS

501	•	Dark blue-green—writing, wreath
501	•	Dark rasberry—tree decorations, wreath, holly berries
535	•	True ash gray—snowman eyes

Christmas Wishes Box

continued from page 122

Row 2: With B, sc in first sc and make color change to A, sc in next 23 sc, sc with A in next sc to point of last yo, complete st with second ball of B. Sc in last sc with B, ch 1, turn. **Rows 3–27:** Continue as established referring to chart *below.* At the end of Row 27, fasten off the yarn. Make 11 more blocks.

Assembly

Using a tapestry needle, sew the blocks together following the diagram *below.* Assemble 4 rows, each with 3 blocks; then sew the rows together.

Border

Round 1: Attach B at upper right corner, ch 1, work 76 sc evenly spaced across top edge and work 3 sc in corner st; work 83 sc evenly spaced along side edge, working 3 sc in next corner; work 76 sc along bottom edge and 3 sc in corner; work 83 sc along opposite side, end rnd with 3 sc in corner; join with sl st to first sc.

Round 2: Ch 1, sc in each sc around and work 3 sc in each corner st; join with sl st to first sc.

Rep Round 2 until border measures 4 inches deep; fasten off B after last sl st is made.

Join A in any sc and work border for 2 inches. Fasten off.

Designed by Stitchworx

Embellished Towels

Shown on pages 112 and 125.

YOU WILL NEED

- Towel set
- Tape measure
- Coordinating fabric, ribbon, trim, and laces
- Sewing threads

INSTRUCTIONS

Fabric and Ribbon Towel Set

To add a fabric border to the bath and hand towels, use a tape measure to find the width of the towel and add 1 inch. Decide on the height of the fabric border; double this number and add 1 inch. Cut a piece of fabric using these measurements.

With right sides facing, fold the fabric in half, aligning the long edges. Sew the short edges together with a ½-inch seam allowance. Trim the seam allowances, turn the border right side out, and press. Baste the top raw edges together. Use contrasting thread to machine-sew a line of decorative stitching close to the long folded edge.

Position and pin the fabric border on the right side of the towel. Cut a ribbon length 1½ inches longer than the width of the towel. Pin the ribbon to the towel, overlapping the raw edges

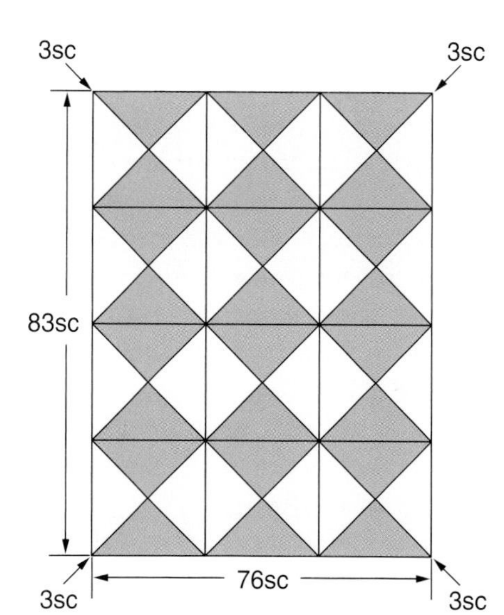

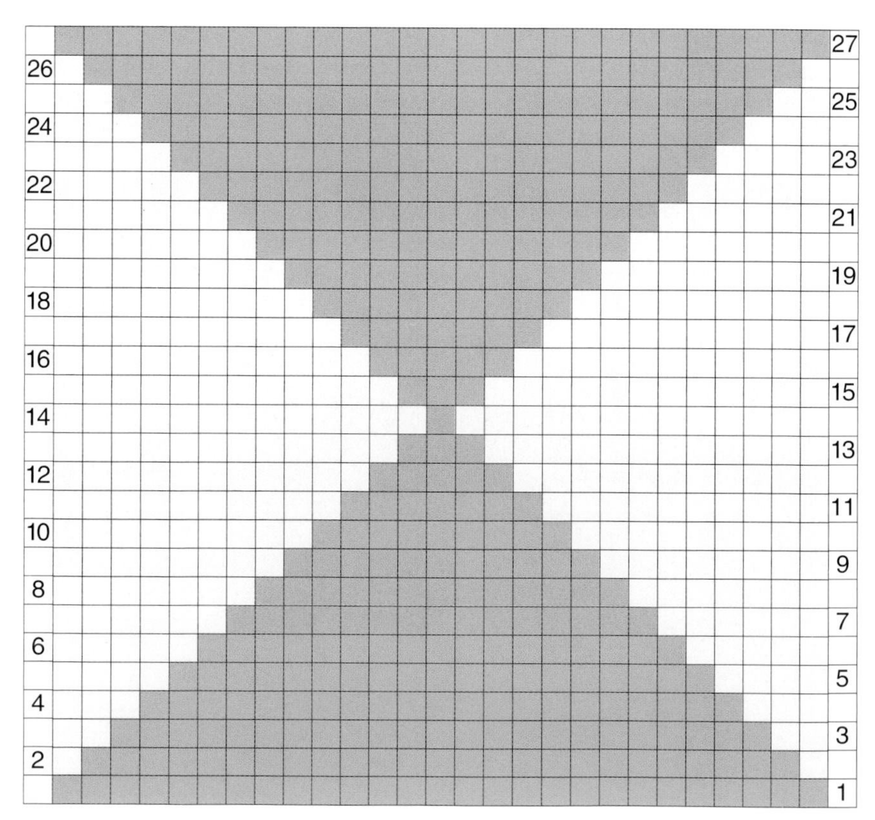

of the fabric border by $\frac{1}{2}$ inch and folding under the ribbon ends so that they are even with the towel edges. Sew close to the ribbon edges, catching the fabric in the stitching. Sew the short edges of the fabric border to the towel. Sew the trim, centering it on the ribbon.

For the washcloth, cut a length of trim slightly longer than the width of the washcloth. Sew the trim over the woven border, folding under the trim ends so that they are even with the cloth edges.

Crochet Lace Towel Set

Cut a length of one or more laces slightly longer than the width of the bath or hand towel. Position the lace on the right side of the towel where desired. Pin the lace in place, folding under the lace ends so that they are even with the towel edges. Sew close to the straight edge of the lace.

For the washcloth, sew the straight edge of the lace to the cloth along all four edges, mitering the corners.

Designed by Mary Jo Hiney

Wool Ministocking

Shown on pages 110 and 127.

MATERIALS

Tracing paper
9×18-inch piece of green felted wool
Scraps of felted wool in gold, red, and blue
Pinking shears; scissors
Size 8 dark gold pearl cotton
Embroidery needle
Four assorted buttons (about $\frac{1}{2}$-inch diameter)

INSTRUCTIONS

Trace the stocking and circle patterns on *page 128* onto tracing paper. Cut out the pattern shapes. Using pinking shears, cut two green stockings from green felted wool. Referring to the pattern, use scissors to cut out the small, medium, and large circle shapes from the assorted colors of felted wool.

Stack the felted wool circles on one stocking half; pin in place. Referring to the photograph *below* and using the embroidery needle and one ply of pearl cotton, straight-stitch the circles to the stocking front. Add a single French knot to the two small circles as indicated on the pattern by a dot. Sew a button to the center of the circles as indicated by an X; then use straight stitches, and carry the stitches over the buttons from the center to the outside edge to hold the button in place. Straight-stitch the embroidered swirls on the stocking front.

Place the stocking front and stocking back together with wrong sides together. Sew the stockings halves together along the sides using tiny straight stitches, leaving the top edge open. If you wish to hang the ministocking on the tree, sew a loop of pearl cotton to the top open edge on the heel side of the stocking.

Designed by Nancy Wyatt

Paper Stocking

Shown below.

YOU WILL NEED

- Tracing paper
- Scrapbook papers: red-and-gold floral and gold-plaid vellum
- Red metallic eyelets: six 1/16-inch and five 1/8- inch
- Eyelet setter
- Sewing machine and coordinating thread
- Making Memories Wire Alphabet in Christmas silver
- Four to six 3/4-inch red costume spangles
- Four to six 1/8-inch silver jump rings
- Needle-nose pliers

INSTRUCTIONS

Trace the design on *page 129* onto tracing paper; cut out the pattern. Cut one stocking shape out of the red-and-gold floral paper and one stocking shape out of the gold-plaid vellum. Fold the top of the red-and-gold floral shape to the wrong side. Fold the top of the vellum shape 1/4-inch lower than the red-and-gold stocking top; pressing it toward the right side.

Using an eyelet setter, attach six 1/16-inch eyelets evenly spaced across the folded top edge of the vellum shape.

Place the wrong side of the vellum stocking shape and the right side of the red-and-gold floral shape together. Using a wide stitch setting on the sewing machine, sew the two shapes together along the side as indicated on the pattern. Use the eyelet setter to attach five 1/8-inch eyelets, evenly spaced along the front of the stocking shape, as indicated on the pattern.

Make a tiny hole in the centers of the spangles. Attach a letter to each spangle. We applied a four-letter name, but you could substitute "noel" for the name. Attach the decorated spangles to the eyelets at the top of the vellum stocking with jump rings; close the jump rings with needle-nose pliers.

Designed by Carrie Topp

Knitted Gift Stocking

Shown on page 110 and opposite.

YOU WILL NEED

- Dale of Norway Heilo yarn:
- 1 50 gram ball, 100 meters/109 yards each: Green #7382, Gold #2537, Navy #5563, and Red #4227
- Size 5 double point needles (dpn)

Gauge: 6 stitches = 1 inch

Special Abbreviations:

K2tog: Knit 2 stitches together (decrease).

P2tog: Purl 2 stitches together (decrease).

SSK: Slip 2 stitches, one at a time knitwise, insert the left-hand needle and knit 2 stitches together (decrease).

INSTRUCTIONS

Seed Stitch Cuff

Using green yarn, cast on 32 stitches. Divide the stitches onto 3 needles. Join and work in the round, taking care not to twist the stitches.

Round 1: Knit 1, purl 1 around.
Round 2: Purl 1, knit 1 around.
Repeat rounds 1–2 two more times.

Leg

Change to gold yarn; knit 4 rounds.
Change to navy yarn; knit 4 rounds.
Change to red yarn; knit 4 rounds.
Change to green yarn; knit 4 rounds.
Change to gold yarn; knit 4 rounds.
Change to navy yarn; knit 4 rounds.
Change to red yarn; knit 4 rounds (34 rounds total, including the 6 rounds of seed stitch for the cuff.

Divide Stitches for Heel

Place 16 stitches on needle #1, 8 stitches on needle #2, and 8 stitches on needle #3. Continue to knit with red for 1 row.

Then change to green for the next 12 rows. Work back and forth on needle #1 as follows:.

Row 1 (right side): *Slip 1, knit 1*, repeat between * across.

Row 2: Slip 1, purl remaining stitches across row.

Repeat these two rows until a total of 13 rows have been completed, ending with a Row 1.

Turn Heel

Continuing with green yarn, work short rows as follows:

Row 1: Purl 10, p2tog, purl 1, turn work.

Row 2: Slip 1, knit 5, k2tog, knit 1, turn work.

Row 3: Slip 1, purl 6, p2tog, purl 1, turn work.

Row 4: Slip 1, knit 7, k2tog, knit 1, turn work.

Row 5: Slip 1, purl 8, p2tog, turn work.

Row 6: Knit 9, k2tog—10 stitches remain.

Gusset

Continuing with green, and using an extra dpn, pick up and knit 8 stitches along the side of the heel, working into the slip stitches on the edge. Combine the instep stitches from the next 2 needles onto one needle. Knit across. Pick up and knit 8 stitches along the other side of the heel. Knit 5 stitches from the last needle. Slip the other half of these stitches onto the first needle. This is now the center back of the heel (there are 13 stitches each on needles #1 and #3; 16 stitches on needle #2)—42 stitches total.

Begin knitting in the round again, and decrease as follows:

Round 1: Still working with green, knit.

Round 2: Knit to last 3 stitches on Needle #1, then k2tog, knit 1. Knit across Needle #2. Then for Needle #3, knit 1, SSK, knit remaining stitches—40 stitches remain.

Round 3: Knit.

Round 4: Change to gold yarn. Knit to last 3 stitches on Needle #1, then K2tog; knit 1. Knit across Needle #2. Then for Needle #3, knit 1, SSK; knit remaining stitches—38 stitches.

Round 5: Knit.

Round 6: Knit to last 3 stitches on Needle #1, then k2tog, knit 1. Knit across Needle #2. Then for Needle #3, knit 1, SSK; knit remaining stitches—36 stitches.

Round 7: Knit.

Round 8: Change to navy yarn. Knit to last 3 stitches on Needle #1, then k2tog; knit 1. Knit across Needle #2. Then for Needle #3, knit 1, SSK; knit remaining stitches—34 stitches.

Round 9: Knit.

Round 10: Knit to last 3 stitches on Needle #1, then k2tog, knit 1. Knit across Needle #2. Then for Needle #3, knit 1, SSK; knit remaining stitches—32 stitches.

Foot

Knit one more round in navy.

Change to red yarn. Knit 4 rounds.

Change to green yarn. Knit 4 rounds.

Change to gold yarn. Knit 4 rounds.

Change to navy yarn. Knit 3 rounds.

Shape Toe

Continue with navy yarn.

Round 1: Knit to last 3 stitches on Needle #1, k2tog, knit 1. On Needle #2 work knit 1, SSK, K to last 3 stitches, K2tog, knit 1. On Needle #3 work knit 1, SSK, knit remaining stitches.

Round 2: Change to red yarn; knit around.

Round 3: Knit to last 3 stitches on Needle #1, k2tog, knit 1. On Needle

#2 work knit 1, SSK, knit to last 3 stitches, k2tog, knit 1. On Needle #3 work knit 1, SSK, knit remaining stitches.

Round 4: Knit.

Round 5: Knit to last 3 stitches on Needle #1, k2tog, knit 1. On Needle #2 work knit 1, SSK, knit to last 3 stitches, k2tog, knit 1. On Needle #3 work knit 1, SSK, knit remaining stitches.

Round 6: Change to green yarn; knit around.

Round 7: Knit to last 3 stitches on Needle #1, k2tog, knit 1. On Needle #2 work knit 1, SSK, knit to last 3 stitches, k2tog, knit 1. On Needle #3 work knit 1, SSK, knit remaining stitches.

Round 8: Knit.

Round 9: Knit to last 3 stitches on Needle #1, k2tog, knit 1. On Needle #2 work knit 1, SSK, knit to last 3 stitches, k2tog, knit 1. On Needle #3 work knit 1, SSK, knit remaining stitches—12 stitches remain.

Toe

Knit the stitches from needle #1 to needle #3—6 stitches on each needle. Graft the stitches together with the Kitchener stitch (see the directions, *top right*).

Finishing

Work a 5-inch-long 3-stitch I-cord, following I-cord instructions, *page 129*. Form a loop with the cord, and use the yarn tails to attach the loop to the inside top of the stocking on the heel side.

Kitchener Stitch

With the wrong sides of the work together, hold the 2 needles with the remaining stitches parallel. Thread a tapestry needle with the yarn tail *insert the tapestry needle knitwise through the first stitch on the front

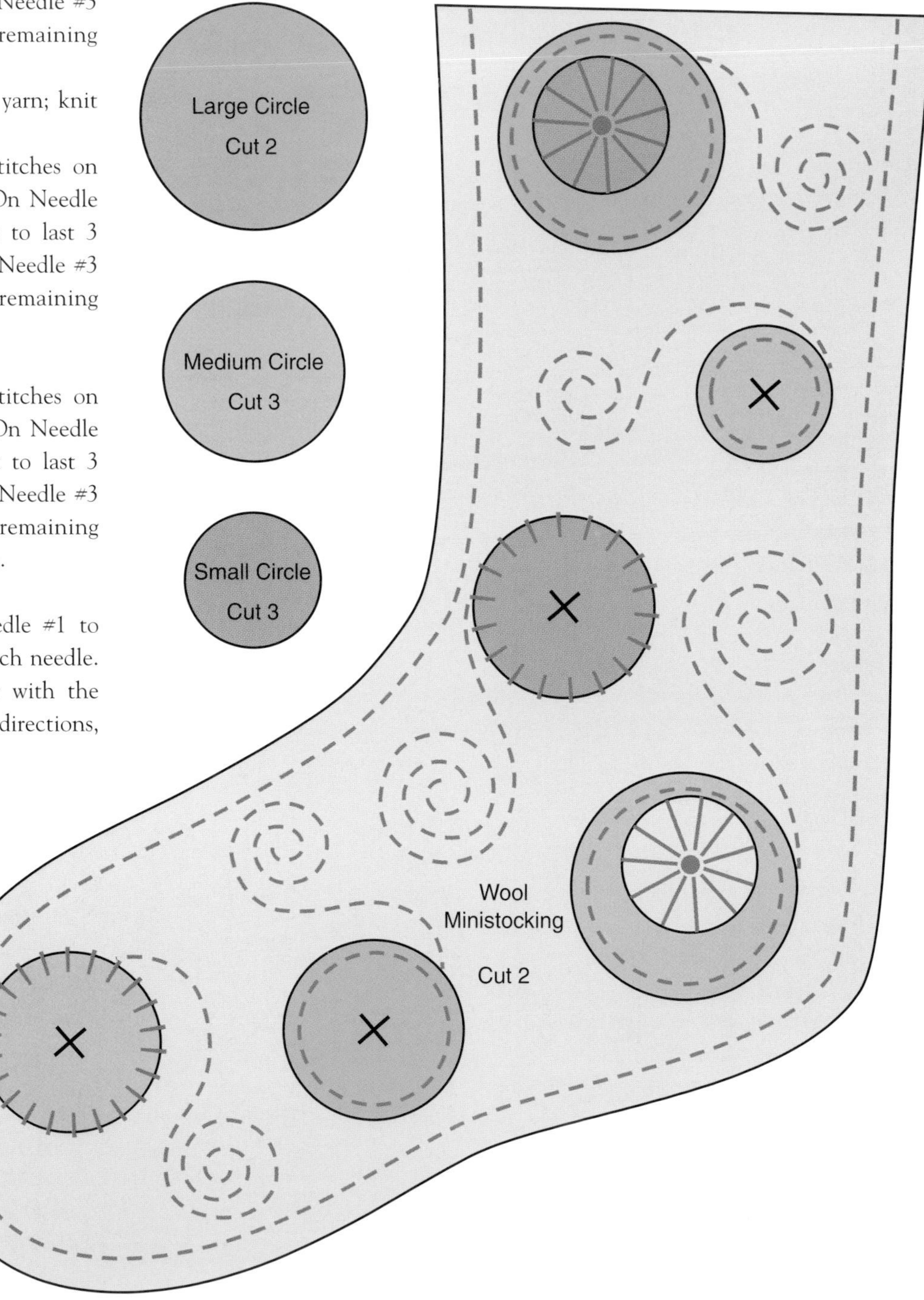

Paper
Stocking

Cut2

needle and let the stitch drop from the needle. Insert the tapestry needle into the second stitch on the front needle purlwise and pull the yarn through, leaving the stitch on the needle. Insert the tapestry needle into the first stitch on the back needle purlwise and let it drop from the needle. Insert the tapestry needle knitwise through the second stitch on the back needle and pull the yarn through, leaving the stitch on the needle.

Repeat from * across until all stitches have been joined. (Refer to the illustration, *below.)* Adjust the tension of the yarn as necessary. Weave in the loose ends.

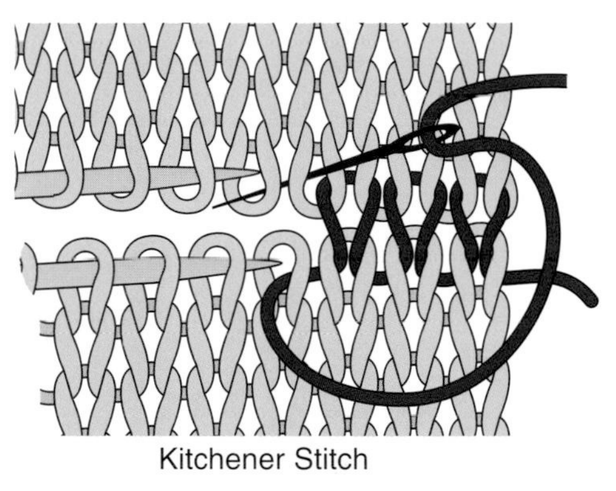

Kitchener Stitch

I-Cord

Cast 3 stitches onto a dpn.

Row 1: Knit; do not turn.

Row 2: Slide the stitches to the other end of the needle. Knit. (Give the yarn a gentle tug at the beginning of each row.) Repeat Row 2 until the cord is the desired length. Bind off, leaving an 8-inch tail.

Designed by Rose Limke

Chocolate Chip-Ginger Cheesecake
(recipe, page 143)

Sugar-and-Spice Pecans (recipe, page 135)

Gifts from Your Pantry

IMAGINE OPENING YOUR CUPBOARD and finding everything you need to make or bake a dozen unique and delicious gifts! Forget making a last-minute dash to the store or trying to substitute on-hand ingredients that just won't work. With our handy list of 20 ultimate holiday pantry ingredients, you're ready to create the yummy gifts your loved ones will remember long after the last crumb is gone. Ready? Turn the page for our ultimate gift-giving pantry list.

Ginger Chocolate Cups (recipe, page 139)

OUR ULTIMATE PANTRY LIST FOR HOMEMADE GIFTS

Grab your pencil and write these ingredients on your next grocery list. It's your ticket to the 12 different food gifts you see on these pages.

1. all-purpose flour
2. granulated sugar
3. powdered sugar
4. brown sugar
5. butter
6. large eggs
7. two-percent milk
8. cream cheese
9. quick-cooking oats
10. baking powder
11. sliced almonds
12. pecan halves
13. semisweet chocolate chips
14. canned pumpkin
15. fresh oranges
16. fresh pears
17. dried cranberries
18. crystallized ginger
19. vanilla
20. pumpkin pie spice

Toffee-Almond Sandies
(recipe, page 135)

Cranberry-Chocolate Chip Cookie Mix

Cranberry-Chocolate Chip Cookie Mix

Prep: 20 minutes

This recipe makes one jar of mix, but you can set up an assembly line and make it several times over. Why not entice your helpers by baking up a batch?

- **¾ cup all-purpose flour**
- **½ teaspoon baking powder**
- **¼ teaspoon salt**
- **⅔ cup sugar**
- **1 cup semisweet chocolate pieces**
- **½ cup dried cranberries**
- **1 cup quick-cooking rolled oats**
- **½ cup chopped pecans**

In a small mixing bowl, stir together flour, baking powder, and salt. In a decorative 1-quart glass jar, layer ingredients in the following order: sugar, chocolate pieces, the flour mixture, cranberries, oats, and pecans. Tap jar gently on the counter to settle each layer before adding the next. Cover the jar and attach baking directions. Store at room temperature for up to 1 month. *Makes 1 jar (about 2 dozen cookies).*

Baking directions: Preheat oven to 350°F. Empty contents of jar into a large mixing bowl. Add ½ cup softened *butter,* 1 slightly beaten *egg,* 1 tablespoon *milk,* and 1 teaspoon *vanilla;* stir until combined. Drop dough by teaspoons about 2 inches apart onto ungreased cookie sheets. Bake for 10 to 12 minutes or until light brown. Transfer cookies to wire racks; cool completely.

Toffee-Almond Sandies

Prep: 25 minutes Bake: 15 minutes per batch
Cool: 1 hour Oven: 325°F

Glue fabric and ribbon onto small gift boxes and fill each with a dozen of these buttery nut balls, as pictured on *page 133*.

- **1 cup butter**
- **½ cup packed brown sugar**
- **1 tablespoon water**
- **1½ teaspoons vanilla**
- **2¼ cups all-purpose flour**
- **1 cup finely chopped sliced almonds**
- **1 cup sifted powdered sugar**

Preheat oven to 325°F. In a large mixing bowl, beat butter with an electric mixer on medium speed for 30 seconds. Add brown sugar. Beat until combined, scraping side of bowl. Beat in the water and vanilla. Beat in as much of the flour as you can with the mixer. Stir in any remaining flour. Stir in almonds.

Shape dough into 1-inch balls. Place balls 1 inch apart on ungreased cookie sheets. Bake for 15 minutes or until bottoms are light brown. Transfer cookies to wire racks; cool completely. If desired, store in an airtight container in the freezer for up to 1 month.

Spoon powdered sugar into a plastic bag. Add cooled or thawed cookies; shake to coat. Arrange in decorative containers for gift giving. *Makes about 48 cookies or four 1-dozen cookie gifts.*

Sugar-and-Spice Pecans

Prep: 10 minutes Bake: 20 minutes
Oven: 325°F

Spruce up tins for these nuts with a little greenery and a holiday decoration, as pictured on *page 131*.

- **Nonstick cooking spray**
- **1 egg white**
- **5 cups pecan halves**
- **¾ cup sugar**
- **2 teaspoons pumpkin pie spice**
- **¼ teaspoon salt**

Preheat oven to 325°F. Lightly coat a 15×10×1-inch baking pan with cooking spray; set aside.

In a large mixing bowl, use a fork to slightly beat egg white. Add pecans; toss gently to coat. In a small bowl, stir together sugar, pumpkin pie spice, and salt. Add to pecans; toss gently to coat.

Spread pecans in the prepared pan. Bake for 20 minutes. Spread on a piece of foil; cool completely. Transfer to airtight decorative containers or resealable plastic bags for gift giving. Store at room temperature for up to 2 weeks. *Makes 7 cups or seven 1-cup nut gifts.*

Creamy Pumpkin Dip

Prep: 15 minutes

Present this dreamy dessert dip with some wafers or fresh pears to slice for delicious dipping.

- **1 8-ounce package cream cheese, softened**
- **1 cup canned pumpkin**
- **⅓ cup sugar**
- **1 tablespoon finely chopped crystallized ginger**
- **1½ teaspoons pumpkin pie spice**
- **1 teaspoon vanilla**

In a medium mixing bowl, beat cream cheese with an electric mixer on low speed for 30 seconds. Beat in pumpkin, sugar, crystallized ginger, pumpkin pie spice, and vanilla. Pack in decorative containers for gift giving. Cover and store in the refrigerator for up to 1 week. *Makes 2½ cups or five ½-cup dip gifts.*

Cranberry-Pear Tart

Prep: 1 hour Bake: 30 minutes Oven: 375°F

Look for vintage platters and plates at antique shops to festively wrap your gift.

- **½ cup packed brown sugar**
- **⅓ cup orange juice**
- **2 teaspoons pumpkin pie spice**
- **8 medium pears, peeled, cored, and thinly sliced**
- **⅔ cup dried cranberries**
- **1 recipe Tart Pastry**

For filling, in a large skillet, combine brown sugar, orange juice, and pumpkin pie spice. Bring to boiling, stirring constantly to dissolve sugar. Add pears and cranberries; reduce heat. Cover and simmer about 5 minutes or until pears are tender. Remove from heat; cool slightly.

Preheat oven to 375°F. Arrange pear slices and berries in crust-lined pans, spooning cooking liquid evenly over fruit.

Bake about 30 minutes or until pastry is golden. Cool tarts in pans on wire racks. Remove sides of tart pans; slide tarts on parchment paper onto serving plates. Wrap for gift giving. *Makes 16 servings or two 8-serving-size tart gifts.*

Tart Pastry: Line the bottoms of two 9-inch tart pans with removable bottoms with parchment paper; set aside. (If you don't have 2 tart pans, wrap and chill half of the dough and cover and chill half of the filling while the first tart bakes and cools.)

In a large mixing bowl, stir together 2½ cups *all-purpose flour* and ½ cup *sugar.* Using a pastry blender, cut 1 cup *cold butter* into flour mixture until pieces are pea-size. In a small mixing bowl, stir together 4 beaten *egg yolks* and 2 tablespoons *cold water.* Using a fork, stir egg yolk mixture into flour mixture. Using your fingers, gently knead the dough just until a ball forms. Divide in half.

On a lightly floured surface, use your hands to slightly flatten 1 portion of dough. Place between 2 sheets of waxed paper. Roll dough from center to edge into an 11-inch circle. Ease circle into one of the prepared pans without stretching. Press into fluted side of tart pan and trim edge. Do not prick pastry. Repeat with remaining dough.

FESTIVE WRAPPINGS FOR FESTIVE FOODS

When you go to the extra effort of making food gifts for friends, you want them to look extra special. Take some cues from our photographs to create simply beautiful gifts. For starters, stock up on a few basic supplies, such as ribbon, tissue paper, holiday fabric, gift tags, colorful pens, greenery, baubles, glitter, a stamp set, and gift bags and boxes.

Ribbon and garlands: Tie around plates or tins or glue onto jar lids or jars.

Fabric: Line or cover boxes, trim jar lids, or gather around your gift and tie at the top.

Greenery: Tuck a sprig under ribbon or sign a leaf with metallic ink for a gift tag.

Christmas baubles: Use in place of bows by attaching to packages or jars.

Bags and boxes: Dress up paper containers with stamped designs, glitter, or cut-outs.

Platters, tins, and jars: Look for unique pieces when at garage sales and flea markets.

Cranberry-Pear Tart

Creamy Pumpkin Dip

Tote along a ready-to-serve gift for the party host and you'll be welcome indeed.

Citrus Pumpkin Bread

Citrus Pumpkin Bread

Prep: 25 minutes Bake: 55 minutes Oven: 350°F

Choose the size you want to give—mini, small, medium, or large loaves.

- **3½ cups all-purpose flour**
- **4 teaspoons baking powder**
- **1½ teaspoons pumpkin pie spice**
- **1 teaspoon salt**
- **1 3-ounce package cream cheese, softened**
- **⅔ cup butter, softened**
- **3 cups sugar**
- **4 eggs**
- **⅔ cup water**
- **1 15-ounce can pumpkin**
- **1 tablespoon finely shredded orange peel**
- **1 recipe Streusel-Nut Topping (optional)**

Preheat oven to 350°F. Grease the bottom and ½ inch up the sides of two 9×5×3-inch, three 8×4×2-inch, four 7½×3½×2-inch, or six 5¾×3×2-inch loaf pans; set aside.

In a large mixing bowl, stir together flour, baking powder, pie spice, and salt; set aside.

In a very large mixing bowl, beat cream cheese and butter with an electric mixer on medium to high speed for 30 seconds. Add sugar; beat until combined. Add eggs; beat until combined.

Alternately add flour mixture and water to sugar mixture, beating on low speed after each addition just until combined. Stir in pumpkin and orange peel until combined. Spoon into prepared pans. If desired, sprinkle with Streusel-Nut Topping.

Bake until a wooden toothpick inserted near centers comes out clean. Allow 55 to 60 minutes for 9-inch pans, 50 to 55 minutes for 8-inch pans, 45 to 50 minutes for 7-inch pans, or 40 to 45 minutes for 5-inch pans.

Cool in pans on wire racks for 10 minutes. Remove from pans. Cool completely on wire racks. Wrap decoratively. Store at room temperature for up to 3 days or in the refrigerator for up to 1 week. *Makes 32 servings or 6 mini, 4 small, 3 medium, or 2 large loaf gifts.*

Streusel-Nut Topping: In a small mixing bowl, stir together ¼ cup packed *brown sugar* and ¼ cup *all-purpose flour*. Using a pastry blender, cut in 2 tablespoons *butter* until mixture resembles coarse crumbs. Stir in ⅓ cup chopped *pecans*.

Ginger Chocolate Cups

Prep: 1 hour Stand: 1 hour

Look for the foil candy cups pictured on page 132 wherever candy-making supplies are sold.

- **1 3-ounce package cream cheese, softened**
- **1 teaspoon vanilla**
- **3¼ cups sifted powdered sugar**
- **1 cup dried cranberries**
- **½ cup coarsely chopped sliced almonds**
- **4 teaspoons finely chopped crystallized ginger**
- **1 12-ounce package semisweet chocolate pieces**
- **1 tablespoon shortening**
- **Sliced almonds and/or crystallized ginger (optional)**

In a large mixing bowl, beat cream cheese and vanilla with an electric mixer on medium speed for 30 seconds. Gradually beat in powdered sugar until combined (mixture may appear dry). Stir in cranberries, chopped almonds, and the 4 teaspoons crystallized ginger. Knead mixture in bowl until it holds together.

Shape the cream cheese mixture into 1-inch or ¾-inch balls. (Keep mixture covered while shaping the balls.) Press balls into small 1½-inch-wide or ½-inch-wide foil or paper candy cups.

In a medium saucepan, melt chocolate and shortening over low heat, stirring frequently. Spoon chocolate over candies in cups. If desired, garnish with additional almonds and/or crystallized ginger. Let stand about 1 hour or until set.

Place the chocolate cups in tightly covered decorative containers for gift giving. Store in the refrigerator for up to 1 week. *Makes about forty-eight 1-inch candies, sixty ¾-inch candies or four or five 1-dozen candy gifts.*

Cranberry-Almond Granola

Prep: 15 minutes Bake: 30 minutes Oven: 325°F

Package in quart-size canning jars with ribbon. For fun, add your own seal with sealing wax.

- **Nonstick cooking spray**
- **3½ cups quick-cooking rolled oats**
- **1 cup sliced almonds**
- **¼ cup butter**
- **½ cup packed brown sugar**
- **1 teaspoon finely shredded orange peel**
- **⅔ cup orange juice**
- **½ teaspoon pumpkin pie spice**
- **¾ cup dried cranberries**

Preheat oven to 325°F. Lightly coat a 15×10×1-inch baking pan with cooking spray; set aside.

In a large mixing bowl, stir together oats and almonds; set aside. In a small saucepan, melt butter; stir in brown sugar, orange peel, orange juice, and pumpkin pie spice. Bring to boiling, stirring to dissolve sugar. Reduce heat; boil gently, uncovered, for 3 minutes. Remove from heat. Pour hot mixture over oat mixture; toss gently to coat.

Cranberry-Almond Granola

Spread the mixture in prepared pan. Bake for 15 minutes; stir. Bake 15 to 20 minutes more or until golden, stirring once. Remove from oven; stir in cranberries. Turn out onto foil; cool.

Transfer granola to decorative airtight containers or resealable plastic bags for gift giving. Store at room temperature for up to 2 weeks. *Makes about 6 cups or two 3-cup granola gifts.*

Ginger-Pear Scones

Prep: 25 minutes Bake: 14 minutes Oven: 400°F

Pair these scones with the Orange-Pear Butter on page 143. Remember to write on your gift tag the directions for warming the scones.

- **2¼ cups all-purpose flour**
- **½ cup quick-cooking rolled oats**
- **¼ cup sugar**
- **1 tablespoon baking powder**
- **¼ teaspoon salt**
- **½ cup butter**
- **2 tablespoons finely chopped crystallized ginger**
- **2 eggs**
- **⅓ cup milk**
- **1 medium pear, peeled, cored, and chopped (¾ cup)**

Preheat oven to 400°F. In a large mixing bowl, stir together flour, oats, sugar, baking powder, and salt. Using a pastry blender, cut in butter until mixture resembles coarse crumbs. Stir in ginger. Make a well in the center; set aside.

In a small bowl, beat eggs; stir in milk and pear. Add to flour mixture; stir just until moistened. Turn dough out onto a lightly floured surface. Knead for 10 to 12 strokes or until nearly smooth. Pat into an 8-inch circle. Cut into 8 wedges.

On an ungreased baking sheet, arrange wedges 1 inch apart. Brush with more milk; sprinkle with more sugar and oats. Bake for 14 to 15 minutes or until golden and a toothpick inserted into centers comes out clean. Transfer to wire racks; cool.

Wrap scones decoratively for gift giving. Attach warming directions. Store at room temperature for up to 3 days. *Makes 8 scones or 1 gift.*

Warming directions: Preheat oven to 350°F. Remove decorative wrap. Place scones on a baking sheet. Bake about 5 minutes or until heated through and tops are slightly crisp.

Ginger-Pear Scones and
Orange-Pear Butter (recipe, page 143)

Cranberry-Chocolate Sauce

Cranberry-Chocolate Sauce

Start to finish: 15 minutes

Spoon the sauce into pretty canning jars and include a gift-wrapped scoop for ice cream.

- **1 cup dried cranberries**
- **¾ cup butter**
- **⅔ cup semisweet chocolate pieces**
- **4 cups sifted powdered sugar**
- **1 cup milk**
- **1 tablespoon vanilla**

In a medium mixing bowl, cover cranberries with *boiling water;* let stand for 5 minutes.

Meanwhile, in a large saucepan, melt butter and chocolate pieces over low heat, stirring constantly. Remove from heat. Add powdered sugar, milk, and vanilla; stir until mixed.

Drain cranberries; stir into chocolate mixture. Spoon chocolate mixture into decorative clean ½-pint jars for gift giving. Cover tightly; attach warming directions. Store in the refrigerator for up to 1 week. *Makes 4 half-pint jars for gifts.*

Warming directions: For sauce in microwave-safe jars, remove lid. Heat in a microwave oven on 100% power (high) for 45 to 60 seconds, stirring once. For sauce in nonmicrowave-safe jars, transfer to a small saucepan; warm over low heat.

Chocolate Chip-Ginger Cheesecake

Prep: 35 minutes Bake: 40 minutes
Cool: 45 minutes Chill: 6 hours Oven: 375°F

Tie a colorful ribbon around the platter as pictured on page 130.

- **3 8-ounce packages cream cheese, softened**
- **1 cup sugar**
- **2 tablespoons all-purpose flour**
- **1 teaspoon vanilla**
- **¼ cup milk**
- **3 eggs, slightly beaten**
- **1 cup regular or miniature semisweet chocolate pieces**
- **¼ cup finely chopped crystallized ginger**
- **1 recipe Ginger Pecan Crust**

Preheat oven to 375°F. For filling, in a large mixing bowl, beat cream cheese, sugar, flour, and vanilla until combined. Beat in milk until smooth. Stir in eggs, chocolate, and ginger.

Pour filling into crust-lined pan. Place pan in a shallow baking pan. Bake until a 2½-inch area around the outside edge appears set when gently shaken. Allow 40 to 45 minutes for an 8-inch pan or about 40 minutes for a 9-inch pan.

Cool in pan on a wire rack for 15 minutes. Using a knife, loosen crust from side of the pan; cool for 30 minutes more. Remove the side of the pan; cool completely on rack. Cover and chill in the refrigerator for at least 6 hours or up to 24 hours. If desired, wrap decoratively for gift giving. *Makes 12 to 16 servings or 1 cheesecake gift.*

Ginger Pecan Crust: In a small mixing bowl, stir together 1¼ cups finely chopped *pecans,* ⅔ cup *all-purpose flour,* and 1 tablespoon *crystallized ginger.* Stir in ⅓ cup melted *butter.* Press onto the bottom and 1½ inches up the side of an ungreased 8- or 9-inch springform pan. Set aside.

Orange-Pear Butter

Prep: 1 hour Cook: 2 hours Process: 5 minutes

Give this healthful butter with a home-baked bread, such as the scones pictured on page 141.

- **4½ pounds pears, cored and quartered (about 14 pears)**
- **3 cups water**
- **2 cups sugar**
- **1 tablespoon finely shredded orange peel**
- **⅓ cup orange juice**
- **1½ teaspoons pumpkin pie spice**

In a 6-quart Dutch oven, combine pears and water. Bring to boiling; reduce heat. Cover and simmer for 30 minutes, stirring occasionally. Press mixture through a food mill or sieve (you should have about 8 cups). Return to Dutch oven.

Stir in sugar, orange peel, orange juice, and pumpkin pie spice. Bring to boiling; reduce heat. Simmer, uncovered, over very low heat for 1½ hours or until very thick, stirring often.

Ladle hot mixture into hot, sterilized half-pint canning jars, leaving ¼-inch head space. Wipe jar rims; adjust lids. Process in a boiling-water canner for 5 minutes (start timing when water returns to boil). Remove jars; cool on racks. If desired, decorate for gift giving. Store in a cool, dark place for up to 1 year. *Makes 4 half-pint jars for gifts.*

Cherry Coconut Candies (recipe, page 154)

Let It Snow!

AS GENTLE FLURRIES of white flakes transform the outdoors into a dreamy winter wonderland, let your holiday baking take a white and creamy turn. With billows of whipped cream, swirls of meringue, curls of white chocolate, and a dusting of sugar here and there, you'll swear that Jack Frost is right by your side. On the next few pages, you'll find all kinds of ways to make your holiday sweets glisten, glimmer, and gleam in blankets of white confection.

Nutty White Chocolate Cake (recipe, page 150)

White Chocolate-Banana Cream Pie (recipe, page 153)

THE GREAT WHITE WAY

Much of the art of whitening belongs to fluffy meringue and whipped cream. Follow the guidelines below and you'll be whipping up swirls and peaks in no time.

Meringues: Soft meringues top lemon pies and baked Alaskas, while hard meringues are used for crusts, cookies, or firm frostings. In either case, start with egg whites at room temperature and use clean metal or glass bowls to get the greatest volume. Depending on your recipe, you can beat egg whites to soft peaks (the tips curl when you lift the beaters) or firm peaks (the tips stand straight).

Whipped cream: Unlike meringue, whipping cream whips best when the cream, beaters, and bowl are chilled first. You'll usually whip cream only until soft peaks form.

Meringue Snowflakes (recipe, page 154)

Frosted Ginger Stars and
Snowflakes on Sticks (in stocking)

Frosted Ginger Stars

Prep: 1 hour Chill: 8 to 24 hours
Bake: 8 minutes per batch Oven: 350°F

Pipe snow-white meringue onto these ginger cookies for a one-of-a-kind designer frosting.

- **½ cup butter, softened**
- **¾ cup granulated sugar**
- **1 teaspoon baking soda**
- **1 teaspoon ground ginger**
- **¼ teaspoon salt**
- **⅛ teaspoon ground cloves**
- **½ cup molasses**
- **¼ cup cold, strong coffee**
- **1 egg**
- **2¾ cups all-purpose flour**
- **1 egg white**
- **¾ cup granulated sugar**
- **9 large marshmallows, cut up**
- **¼ cup water**
- **½ teaspoon white vinegar**
- **1 cup sifted powdered sugar**

In a large mixing bowl, beat butter with an electric mixer on medium to high speed for 30 seconds. Add ¾ cup granulated sugar, baking soda, ginger, salt, and cloves. Beat until combined, scraping the side of the bowl occasionally. Beat in molasses, coffee, and egg. Beat in as much of the flour as you can with the mixer. Stir in any remaining flour. Divide dough in half. Cover and chill the dough in the refrigerator for at least 8 hours or up to 24 hours.

Preheat oven to 350°F. On a lightly floured surface, roll dough, half at a time, to ¼-inch thickness. Using a 2½-inch star or other cookie cutters, cut into desired shapes. On ungreased cookie sheets, arrange cookies 1 inch apart. Bake about 8 minutes or until edges are light brown. Cool on cookie sheets for 1 minute. Transfer to wire racks; cool completely.

For meringue frosting, let egg white stand at room temperature for 30 minutes. Meanwhile, in the top of a double boiler, combine ¾ cup sugar, marshmallows, water, and vinegar; place over boiling water (upper pan should not touch water). Cook, stirring constantly, until the marshmallows are melted. Beat egg white with an electric mixer on high speed until stiff peaks form (tips stand straight). Beat into the marshmallow mixture. Cook, beating constantly, for 5 minutes.

Remove from heat; add powdered sugar. Beat until smooth. Pipe frosting onto cookies. Let cookies stand until frosting becomes firm. Store, covered, at room temperature for up to 3 days. *Makes about 48 cookies.*

Snowflakes on Sticks

Prep: 30 minutes Bake: 15 minutes per batch
Oven: 325°F

A sprinkling of coarse sugar sparkles like new-fallen snow. For fun, try some colored sugar, too.

- **2¼ cups all-purpose flour**
- **½ cup granulated sugar**
- **2 teaspoons finely shredded orange, lemon, or lime peel**
- **1 cup butter**
- **1 tablespoon milk**
- **16 lollipop sticks**
- **Milk**
- **Edible glitter, plain or colored coarse sugar, or sifted powdered sugar**
- **Granulated sugar**

In a medium mixing bowl, stir together flour, the ½ cup sugar, and orange, lemon, or lime peel. Using a pastry blender, cut in butter until mixture resembles fine crumbs and starts to cling. Stir in the 1 tablespoon milk. Form mixture into a ball and knead until smooth. Divide dough in half.

Preheat oven to 325°F. On a lightly floured surface, roll dough to ½-inch thickness. Using a 3- to 4-inch snowflake cookie cutter, cut dough into shapes. On an ungreased cookie sheet, arrange cookies about 2 inches apart. Insert a lollipop stick at least 1 inch into each cookie. If desired, use a knife or an hors d'oeuvre cutter to make ¼-inch-deep impressions in cookies.

Brush tops of cookies with additional milk. If using edible glitter, stir together equal proportions of glitter and additional granulated sugar. Sprinkle glitter mixture, coarse sugar, or powdered sugar onto cookies.

Bake for 15 minutes or until very light brown around edges. Cool on cookie sheet for 1 minute. Using a spatula, carefully transfer cookies to a wire rack; cool completely. Store, covered, at room temperature up to 3 days. *Makes 16 cookies.*

Macadamia-Vanilla Bark

Start to finish: 15 minutes

Chunky white macadamia nuts make this candy look like a snow-covered rocky road!

1 pound vanilla-flavored candy coating
3/4 cup finely chopped macadamia nuts or crushed candy canes or striped round peppermint candies (about 5 ounces or 28 candies)

Line a cookie sheet with waxed paper; set aside. In a large microwave-safe bowl, heat candy coating, uncovered, on 100% power (high) for 4 to 6 minutes, stirring after every minute until soft enough to stir smooth. (Or, in a large saucepan, heat candy coating over low heat until melted, stirring constantly.)

If desired, set aside *1/4 cup* of the nuts. Stir remaining nuts into melted candy coating. Spread onto a baking sheet. If desired, sprinkle with reserved nuts. Cool; break into pieces. Store, covered, in the refrigerator for up to 2 weeks. *Makes 1 pound (about 16 pieces).*

Nutty White Chocolate Cake

Prep: 30 minutes Bake: 25 minutes Oven: 350°F

Swirls of creamy white chocolate frosting coat three white chocolate cake layers, all topped with a crest of white chocolate curls, as pictured on page 145.

1 1/2 cups butter
3/4 cup water
4 ounces white baking bar, chopped
1 1/2 cups buttermilk or sour milk*
4 eggs, slightly beaten
3/4 cup toasted chopped pecans
3 1/2 cups all-purpose flour
2 1/4 cups granulated sugar
3/4 cup flaked coconut
1 teaspoon baking soda
1 teaspoon baking powder
1 recipe White Chocolate Frosting
White chocolate curls (optional)

Preheat oven to 350°F. Grease and flour three 9×1 1/2-inch round baking pans; set aside. (If you only have one or two 9-inch pans, cover and save the remaining batter in the refrigerator until you can wash and reuse the pan.)

In a large saucepan, bring butter and water to boiling, stirring constantly. Remove from heat. Add white baking bar; stir until melted. Stir in buttermilk and eggs.

In a small mixing bowl, stir together pecans and *1/2 cup* of the flour; set aside.

In a very large mixing bowl, stir together the remaining *3 cups* flour, the sugar, coconut, baking soda, and baking powder. Stir in egg mixture. Fold in pecan mixture. Divide batter among pans.

Bake for 25 to 30 minutes or until a wooden toothpick inserted near the center of each layer comes out clean. Cool cake layers in pans on wire racks for 10 minutes. Remove cakes from pans; cool completely on wire racks.

To assemble, place one cake layer on a serving platter. Spread with *1/2 cup* of the White Chocolate Frosting. Repeat with a second cake layer and another *1/2 cup* frosting. Top with remaining cake layer. Frost the top and sides with remaining frosting. If desired, garnish the top with white chocolate curls. Store any leftover cake, covered, in the refrigerator for up to 3 days. *Makes 16 servings.*

White Chocolate Frosting: In a small saucepan, melt 4 ounces chopped *white baking bar* over low heat. Cool for 10 minutes. In a large mixing bowl, combine 1/2 cup softened *butter* and one 8-ounce package plus one 3-ounce package softened *cream cheese.* Beat with an electric mixer on medium speed until combined. Beat in melted baking bar. Gradually add 6 cups sifted *powdered sugar,* beating until smooth.

****Note:*** To make 1 1/2 cups sour milk, place 4 1/2 teaspoons *lemon juice* or *vinegar* in a glass measuring cup. Add enough *milk* to make 1 1/2 cups liquid; stir. Let stand for 5 minutes before using the sour milk in a recipe.

Macadamia-Vanilla Bark

Frosty Baked Alaska

Frosty Baked Alaskas

Prep: 25 minutes Freeze: 2 to 24 hours
Bake: 3 minutes Oven: 450°F

Luscious peaks of meringue curl around frozen ice cream and cake. Sprinkle a light shower of snowy powdered sugar onto the plates before serving.

- **6 slices loaf sponge cake or pound cake cut ½ to ¾ inch thick**
- **3 to 6 teaspoons desired flavor liqueur or orange juice***
- **6 scoops desired flavor ice cream***
- **¾ cup water**
- **1½ cups sifted powdered sugar**
- **¼ cup meringue powder**
- **Sifted powdered sugar (optional)**

If desired, use a 3-inch round cookie cutter to cut cake slices into rounds. On an ungreased baking sheet, arrange cake slices. Sprinkle with liqueur or orange juice. Place a scoop of ice cream on each. Cover and freeze for at least 2 hours or up to 24 hours.

Preheat oven to 450°F. For meringue, in a large mixing bowl, stir together *½ cup* of the powdered sugar and the meringue powder. Stir in the water. Beat with an electric mixer on high speed for 5 minutes. Gradually beat in the remaining *1 cup* powdered sugar.

Spread the meringue onto each cake and ice cream stack. Bake for 3 minutes or until top of meringue is golden.

If desired, sprinkle 6 dessert plates with additional powdered sugar. Place meringue-covered stacks on dessert plates; serve immediately. *Makes 6 servings.*

***Note:** Think about matching liqueurs and ice creams, such as amaretto with chocolate-almond ice cream, coffee liqueur with mocha ice cream, chambord with strawberry ice cream, or crème de menthe with chocolate-mint ice cream.

White Chocolate-Banana Cream Pie

Prep: 30 minutes Bake: 5 minutes
Chill: 4 to 24 hours Oven: 375°F

Drifts of billowy whipped cream blanket the yummy layers underneath. Pictured on page 146.

- **½ cup granulated sugar**
- **¼ cup cornstarch**
- **2½ cups milk**
- **4 egg yolks, slightly beaten**
- **4 ounces white chocolate baking squares, finely chopped**
- **1 teaspoon vanilla**
- **4 medium bananas, sliced (about 3 cups)**
- **1 recipe Vanilla Wafer Crust**
- **1 cup whipping cream**
- **2 tablespoons sifted powdered sugar**
- **Banana slices (optional)**

For filling, in a medium saucepan, stir together granulated sugar and cornstarch. Stir in milk. Cook and stir over medium heat until thickened and bubbly. Cook and stir for 2 minutes more. Remove from heat.

Gradually stir about *1 cup* of the hot mixture into beaten egg yolks, stirring constantly. Pour egg yolk mixture into remaining hot mixture in saucepan. Bring to a gentle boil. Cook and stir for 2 minutes more. Remove saucepan from heat. Stir in white chocolate and *½ teaspoon* of the vanilla; heat and stir until chocolate is melted.

Arrange the slices from 2 bananas in cooled Vanilla Wafer Crust. Spread with *half* of the white chocolate filling. Top with remaining banana slices and filling. Cover and chill in the refrigerator for at least 4 hours or up to 24 hours.

Before serving, in a chilled medium mixing bowl, combine whipping cream, powdered sugar, and the remaining *½ teaspoon* vanilla. Beat with chilled beaters of an electric mixer on medium speed until soft peaks form (tips curl). Spread whipped cream mixture onto pie. If desired, top with additional banana slices. *Makes 10 servings.*

Vanilla Wafer Crust: Preheat oven to 375°F. In a small mixing bowl, combine 1⅓ cups crushed *vanilla wafers* and ⅓ cup melted *butter;* toss gently to mix. Spread into a 9-inch pie plate. Press onto bottom and up the side to form a firm, even crust. Bake for 5 minutes. Cool on wire rack.

Coconut Eggnog

Prep: 20 minutes Chill: 3 hours

Top each frothy serving with a soft and dreamy pillow of sweetened whipped cream.

- **3 cups milk**
- **6 egg yolks, beaten**
- **1 15- to 16-ounce can cream of coconut**
- **½ cup light rum**
- **2 teaspoons vanilla**
- **½ cup whipping cream**
- **1 tablespoon sugar**

In a medium saucepan, stir together milk and egg yolks. Cook and stir just until mixture comes to boil; remove from heat. Immediately stir in cream of coconut, rum, and vanilla. Transfer to a pitcher or punch bowl. Cover and chill in the refrigerator about 3 hours or until cold.

To serve, in a chilled medium mixing bowl, beat cream and sugar with chilled beaters of an electric mixer on medium speed until soft peaks form (tips curl). Serve over eggnog. *Makes ten 4-ounce servings.*

Meringue Snowflakes

Prep: 1 hour Bake/dry: 1 hour Oven: 300°F

Delicate and crisp, these feathery snowflakes melt on your tongue just like the real thing. Pictured on page 147.

- **2 egg whites**
- **¼ teaspoon cream of tartar**
- **1⅓ cups sifted powdered sugar**
- **Desired food coloring (optional)**
- **Plain or colored coarse sugar or decorating candies**

Let egg whites stand at room temperature for 30 minutes. Line 3 cookie sheets with parchment paper; set aside.

Preheat oven to 300°F. In a medium mixing bowl, beat egg whites and cream of tartar with an electric mixer on high speed until soft peaks form (tips curl). Add powdered sugar, 1 tablespoon at a time, beating well after each addition. If desired, add food coloring. Beat mixture for 7 minutes on high speed. (The mixture should be very thick and glossy, but may not be stiff.)

Spoon mixture into a decorating bag fitted with a medium star tip (1/16-inch opening). Making lines about ¼ inch thick, pipe 4- to 5-inch snowflake shapes about 2 inches apart onto prepared cookie sheets. Sprinkle with coarse sugar or candies.

Place the cookie sheets in the oven. Turn off oven. Let meringues dry in the oven with the door closed about 1 hour or until dry and crisp but still white. Cool on cookie sheets on wire racks.

Carefully cut parchment paper around snowflakes. Using your hands, gently peel parchment away from snowflakes. Store in an airtight container in a cool, dry place for up to 1 week. *Makes 10 to 12 cookies.*

Cherry Coconut Candies

Prep: 20 minutes Chill: 15 minutes + 20 minutes

These lacy mounds offer a mountain of flavor, capped with candied cherry. Pictured on page 144.

- **2 teaspoons butter**
- **3 tablespoons water**
- **1 teaspoon vanilla**
- **2 cups sifted powdered sugar**
- **½ cup nonfat dry milk powder**
- **1 7-ounce package (2⅔ cups) flaked coconut**
- **9 candied cherries, quartered**
- **6 ounces vanilla-favored candy coating**
- **1 teaspoon shortening**
- **Sifted powdered sugar (optional)**

In a large saucepan, melt butter over low heat. Remove from heat. Stir in water and vanilla.

In a medium mixing bowl, combine the 2 cups powdered sugar and nonfat dry milk powder. Add to the butter mixture; stir until combined. Add coconut; stir until coated.

Drop mixture by small teaspoonfuls onto a waxed-paper-lined baking sheet. Top candies with cherry pieces. Chill in the refrigerator for 15 minutes.

Meanwhile, in a small saucepan, melt candy coating and shortening over very low heat, stirring constantly. Cool slightly.

Drizzle coating over candies. Chill in the refrigerator for 20 minutes more or until firm. Store, covered, in the refrigerator for up to 2 weeks. If desired, sprinkle with powdered sugar before serving. *Makes about 36 candies.*

Coconut Eggnog

Crafting Basics

Crochet

Chain One Stitch

Make a slipknot about 4" from the end of the yarn and slip the loop onto the crochet hook. Weave the yarn loosely under the little finger, over the ring finger, under the third finger, and over the index finger of your left hand; grasp the tail of the yarn between the thumb and third finger. Hold the hook (with the slipknot on it) in your right hand, slip it under the yarn; use the hook to pull it through the loop to complete one chain stitch. Continue chain-stitching the desired number of stitches to make a foundation chain.

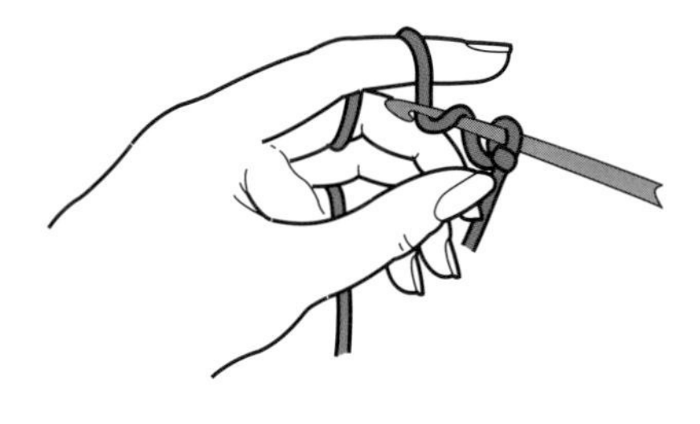

Single Crochet

Step 1: At the beginning of a row, insert your crochet hook into the second chain from the hook.

Steps 2 and 3: Slip the hook under the yarn, and then use the hook to pull it through the chain. This is called "yarn over" (or "yarn over hook") and is abbreviated as "yo." Notice that there are two loops on the hook.

Steps 4 and 5: Yarn over again, and then pull the loop completely through the two loops on the hook. You have just completed a single crochet. To work the next single crochet, insert your hook into the next chain, and repeat Steps 2–5.

Double Crochet

Step 1: At the beginning of a row, slip the hook under the yarn (yarn over), and insert the hook into the fourth chain from the hook.

Step 2: Yarn over again, and pull the loop through the stitch. There are three loops on the hook.

Step 3: Yarn over, and pull the loop completely through the first two loops on the hook. Notice that two loops remain on the hook.

Steps 4 and 5: Yarn over once more, and pull the loop through the remaining two loops on the hook. One loop remains on the hook. You have just completed a double crochet. To work the next double crochet, yarn over and insert your hook into the next chain; repeat Steps 2-5.

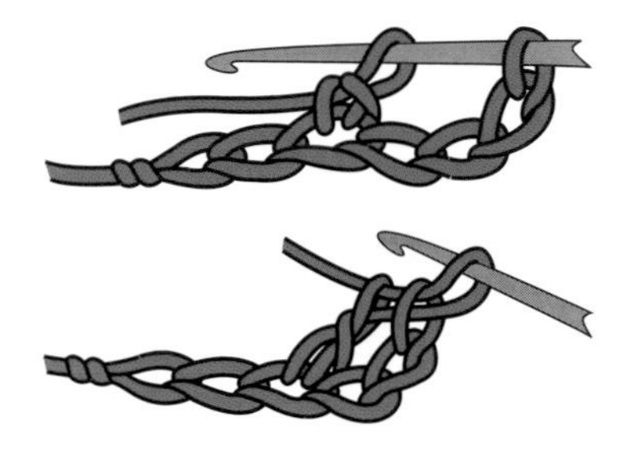

Slip Stitch

Step 1: Insert your hook into a stitch. Yarn over, and pull the yarn through the stitch and through the loop on the hook. You've completed a slip stitch.

Cross-Stitch

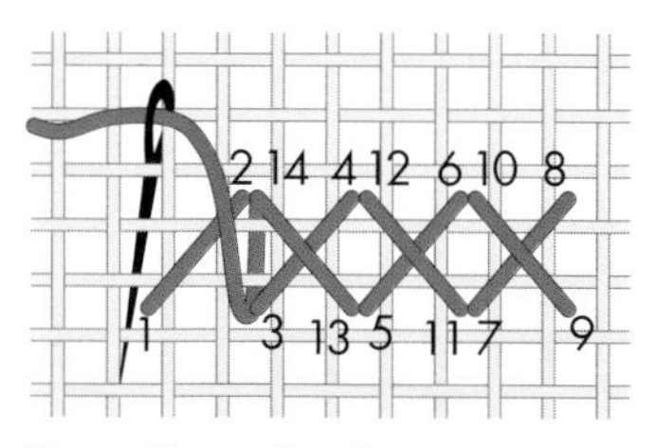

Basic Cross-Stitch

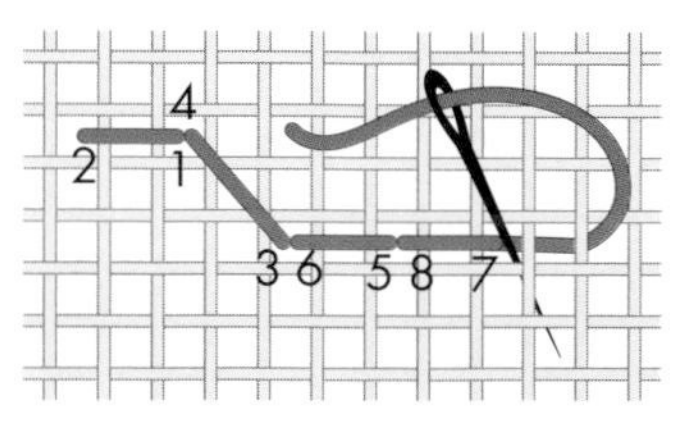

Backstitch

Knitting

Casting On

Step 1: Make a slipknot on the left needle.

Step 2: Working into the loop of the knot, knit a stitch; transfer it to the left needle.

Step 3: Insert right needle between the last 2 stitches. Knit a stitch and transfer it to left needle. Repeat this step for each additional stitch.

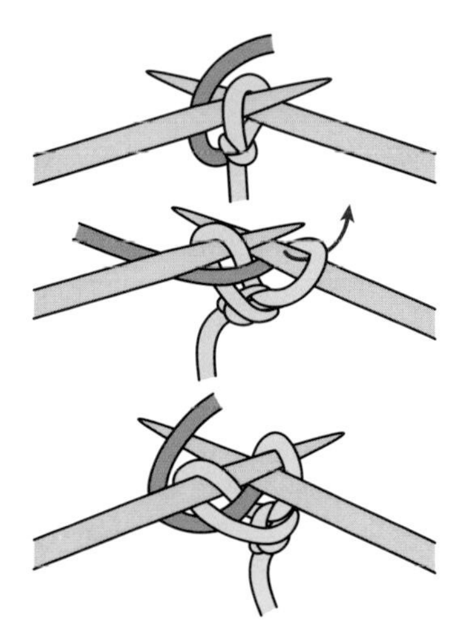

Knit Stitch

Step 1: Insert the right-hand needle from front to back into the first stitch on the left-hand needle. Notice that the right-hand needle is behind the left-hand needle.

Step 2: Form a loop by wrapping the yarn under and around the right-hand needle.

Step 3: Pull the loop through the stitch so the loop is in front of the work.

Step 4: Slip the first or "old" knit stitch over and off the tip of the left-hand needle.

M1 (make one stitch)

This increase is worked by lifting the horizontal thread lying between the needles and placing it onto the left needle. Work the new stitch through the back loop.

Purl Stitch

Step 1: With yarn in front of the work, put the right-hand needle from back to front into the first stitch on the left-hand needle.

Step 2: Form a loop by wrapping the yarn on top of and around the right-hand needle.

Step 3: Pull the loop through the stitch to make a new purl stitch.

Step 4: Slip the first or "old" purl stitch over and off the tip of the left-hand needle.

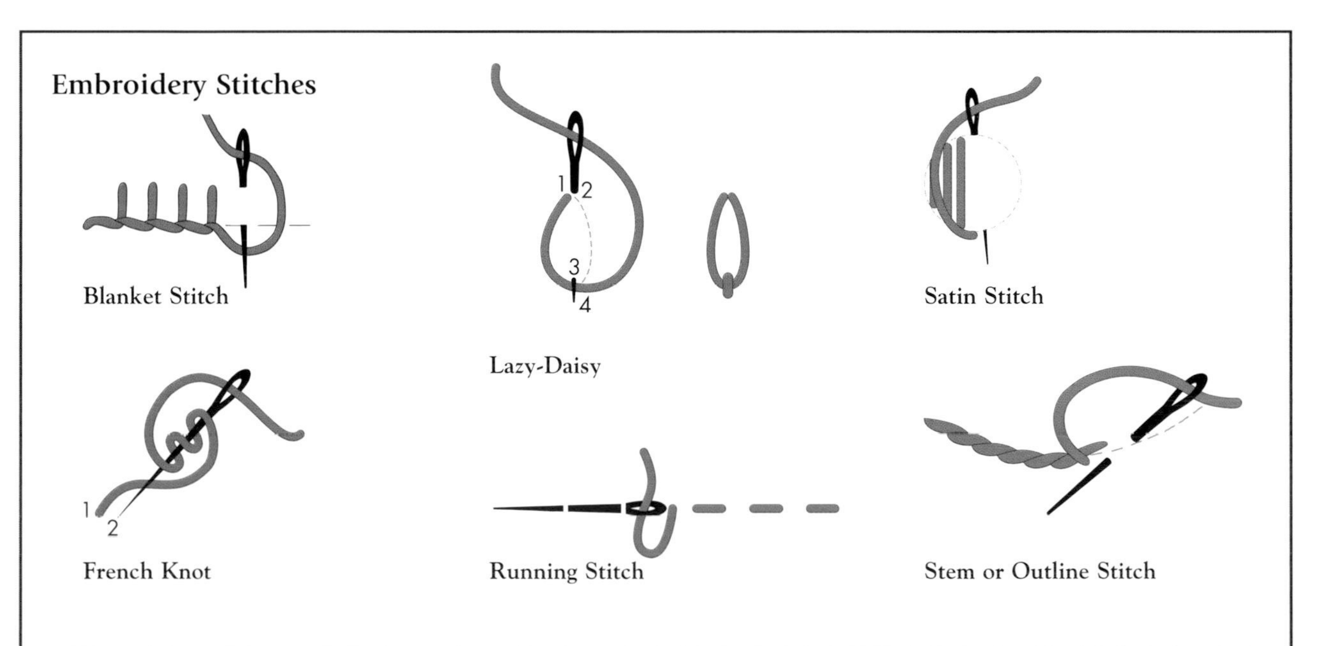

Sources

Materials used in the projects are listed under the chapter headings below. Many of these materials are available at your local crafts and art stores. A contact list for the suppliers of these materials appears after the chapter listings. The suppliers are listed in alphabetical order. For a retailer near you, contact the suppliers or manufacturers listed.

Holly and Berries, *pages 6–13:*
Iced Himalayan Spruce prelit Christmas tree XV9362/90L, Iced Himalayan Spruce garland XZ6382-12L, Iced Himalayan Spruce wreath XV5382/30, and Holly and Berry sprays—**Aldik**
Ornaments and giftware: Vintage Rose Spray #488669, Silver Sugar and Creamer #459201, Silver Teapot #459225, Silver Trays #405079, Silver Cup and Saucer #459218, Silver Coffeepot #405093, Silver Spoon with Crystal Drops #405055, Glass Rose-and-Leaf Garland #527627, Clip-on Cardinals #462959, and Picture Frame #529102—**Seasons of Cannon Falls by Midwest**

Earth Angels, *pages 14–31:*
Iced Himalayan Spruce prelit Christmas tree XV9362/90L—**Aldik**
Green Glass Leaf Garland #466087, Clip-on Floral Hat Spray #546314, Stars #538357, Mirror Garland #413531, Icy White Beaded Buds Sprays #413517, Juniper Picks #536308, and Copper Garland #467411—**Seasons of Cannon Falls by Midwest**
2-inch round heart ornaments—**Department 56**
Wool felt—**National Nonwovens**
Papers—**Anna Griffin Inc.**
Bias-cut silk ribbon—**Hanah Silk from Artemis**
William Morris stained-glass coloring book—**Dover Publications, Inc.**
Fringe, trims, and Dylon Cold Water Dye—**Prym-Dritz Corporation**
Mod Podge—**Plaid Enterprises**

A Way with Wreaths, *pages 32–45:*
Snowflake yarn—**Herrschners**
Styrofoam—**Dow Chemical**
Colored wire—**Artistic Wire**
Fun Wire plastic-covered wire—**Toner Plastics, Inc.**
Wool felt—**National Nonwovens**
Vintage mica snow—**Mica Snow**
Ribbon trims—**Marcel Schurman Co.**
Spray paint—**Krylon**
Ribbon (terra-cotta ball, tea, and baby wreaths)—**C.M. Offray & Son, Inc.**
Ribbon (snowman wreath)—**Midori**
Baby Boy Outfit by Jolee's Boutique—**EK Success**

Red-and-White Whimsy, *pages 46–57:*
Iced Himalayan Spruce prelit Christmas tree XV9362/90L, Iced Himalayan Spruce wreath XV5382/30—**Aldik**
Small Frosted White Kugel #469736; Large Frosted White Kugel #469705; Red Teardrop, Heart, and Ball Ornaments #246108; Ball and Drop Peppermint Stripe Ornaments #462294; Red Ball Garland #471197; Twisted Icicle Drop Ornament #530351; and Beaded Snowflakes #408407—**Seasons of Cannon Falls by Midwest**
Flowers, trims, stamens, and leaves—**Lina G**
Candy cane brush letter stickers (greetings garland)—**EK Success**
Wool felt—**National Nonwovens**
Red-and-white ribbon—**Nashville Wraps**
Lace stickers—**Mrs. Grossman's**

Cavity-Free Christmas, *pages 68-79:*
Sculpey Premo polymer clay (all ornaments)—**Polyform Products Co.**
Wool felt—**National Nonwovens**
Jumbo rickrack—**Wrights**
2-inch round ornaments—**Department 56**

Plentiful Christmas, *pages 80–99:*
Silver Spruce prelit tree XV9323/90L—**Aldik**
Glass Kugel Ornaments #529058, Pewter-Finish Glass Ornaments #397503, Oak Leaf and Berry Spray #469675, Velvet Oak Pick #525548, Oak Leaf and Berry Garland #469682, and Stag's Head Pick #547083—**Seasons of Cannon Falls by Midwest**
Fresh pomegranates—**Pom Wonderful**
Trims, vintage cherry clusters, acorn pips—**Lina G**
Styrofoam—**Dow Chemical**
Eyelets —**Making Memories**
Rayon floss—**DMC Corporation**
Embossed paper—**Anna Griffin**

Creative Cards & Gift Wrap, *pages 100–109:*
Ribbon—**Midori**

Gifts for Giving, *pages 110–129:*
Wool felt—**National Nonwovens**
Heilo yarn—**Dale of Norway**
Felted wool—**Rosebud's Cottage**
Homespun yarn—**Lion Brand Yarn Co.**
Needlework box—**Sudberry House**
Wire alphabet and eyelets—**Making Memories**

SUPPLIERS

Aldik, 800/442-5345; www.aldik.com
Anna Griffin Inc., 733 Lambert Drive, Atlanta, GA 30324; www.annagriffin.com
Artistic Wire, 630/530-7567; www.artisticwire.com
C.M. Offray & Son, Inc., www.offray.com
Dale of Norway, www.daleofnorway.com
Department 56, www.department56.com
DMC Corporation, 973/589-0606; www.dmc-usa.com
Dover Publications, Inc., 31 East 2nd Street, Mineola, NY 11501; www.doverpublications.com
Dow Chemical, Styrofoam Brand products, www.styrofoamcrafts.com
EK Success, 800/524-1349; www.eksuccess.com
Hanah Silk from Artemis, 179 High Street, South Portland, ME 04106; 888/233-5187; www.artemisinc.com
Herrschners, www.herrschners.com
Krylon, 800/457-9566; www.krylon.com
Lina G, 468 Morro Bay Blvd., Morro Bay, CA 93442; www.trimsandribbons.com
Lion Brand Yarn Co., 800/258-9276; www.lionbrandyarn.com
Making Memories, 801/294-0430; www.makingmemories.com
Marcel Schurman Co., 800/333-6724; www.schurman.com
Mica Snow, 949/581-MICA(6422); www.micasnow.com
Midori, www.midoriribbon.com
Mrs. Grossman's, 800/429-4549; www.mrsgrossmans.com
Nashville Wraps, www.nashvillewraps.com
National Nonwovens, 180 Pleasant Street, P.O. Box 150, Easthampton, MA 01027; 800/333-3469, www.woolfelt.com
Plaid Enterprises, 800/842-4197; www.plaidonline.com
Polyform Products Co., www.sculpey.com
Pom Wonderful, www.pomwonderful.com
Prym-Dritz Corporation, 864/576-5050; www.dritz.com
Rosebud's Cottage, 2580 Seventh Ave., North St. Paul, MN 55109; phone 651/426-1885 or fax 651/426-1879
Seasons of Cannon Falls by Midwest, 800/776-2075; www.midwestofcannonfalls.com
Sudberry House, 860/739-6951; www.sudberry.com
Toner Plastics, Inc., www.tonerplastics.com
Wrights, 800/628-9362; www.wrights.com

Better Homes and Gardens® Creative Collection™

CHRISTMAS
FROM THE HEART®

Director, Editorial Administration
Michael L. Maine

Editor-in-Chief
Beverly Rivers

Editorial Manager Ann Blevins
Art Director Brenda Drake Lesch

Managing Editor
Karman Wittry Hotchkiss

Senior Editor	Nancy Wyatt
Associate Art Director	Shawn Roorda
Senior Food Editor	Julia Martinusen
Copy Chief	Mary Heaton
Editorial Assistant	Lori Eggers
Contributing Proofreader	Katherine C. Nugent
Contributing Writers	Rhonda Matus, Heidi Palkovic
Contributing Photographers	Marcia Cameron (96-97, 99, 101), Bill Hopkins (14–19, 76–81, 110–117), Pete Krumhardt (32–39, 75), Scott Little (6–11, 64, 130–153), Andy Lyons (46–51, 68–73, 160), Steve Struse (98, 100), Dean Tanner (20–21, 24, 27–28, 31, 52–57, 82, 86, 88, 93-94, 115, 118, 120–122, 125)
Contributing Food Stylists	Jill Lust, Dianna Nolin, Charles Worthington
Contributing Illustrator	Glenda Aldrich

Vice President, Publishing Director
William R. Reed

Group Publisher	Maureen Ruth
Cons. Prod. Sr. Marketing Manager	Steve Swanson
Cons. Prod. Marketing Manager	Karrie Nelson
Business Director	Christy Light
Business Manager	Jie Lin
Director, Production	Douglas M. Johnston
Books Production Managers	Pam Kvitne, Marjorie J. Schenkelberg, Rick von Holdt
Assistant to the Publisher	Cheryl Eckert

MEREDITH PUBLISHING GROUP

Publishing Group President	Stephen M. Lacy
Magazine Group President	Jerry Kaplan
Corporate Solutions	Michael Brownstein
Creative Services	Ellen de Lathouder
Manufacturing	Bruce Heston
Consumer Marketing	Karla Jeffries
Finance and Administration	Max Runciman

Chairman and CEO William T. Kerr

Chairman of the Executive Committee E.T. Meredith III

For editorial questions, please write:

BETTER HOMES AND GARDENS®
Christmas From The Heart®, Volume 12
1716 Locust Street, Des Moines, IA 50309-3023.

Printing Number and Year: 5 4 3 2 1 07 06 05 04 03
ISSN: 1081-4698 ISBN: 0-696 21618-3

From home to home, and heart to heart,
From one place to another.
The warmth and joy of Christmas
Bring us closer to each other.

—Emily Matthews